Faiths and Festivals

Martin Palmer

Ward Lock Educational

First published 1984
by Ward Lock Educational Co Ltd
47 Marylebone Lane
London W1M 6AX

A Ling Kee Company

Reprinted 1988

British Library Cataloguing in Publication Data

Palmer, Martin
    Faiths and festivals.
    1. Religious calendars
    I. Title
    291.3′6   BL 590

    ISBN 0-7062-4293-9

Designed by Peter Tucker.
Typeset in Century Schoolbook
by Dorchester Typesetting Group Limited.
Printed in Hong Kong.

Preface

THIS BOOK is about stories – some of the oldest and most powerful stories in the world which have been told for hundreds and thousands of years. Their fascination lies not just in their age and history, but in the religious insights which they express. These are the tales, the myths and epics which have shaped the great civilizations of the world and which contain extraordinary power to this day. In these tales, the voices of the gods, of God, of angels and of superheroes echo down from the past to shape our present and possibly to foretell our future.

One of the oldest ways in which people have entertained each other is by telling stories. And the best time to do this is when they are gathered for a special occasion – such as a festival or a family celebration. Thus it is that all the major religious festivals are closely linked to stories, which capture their fundamental point and purpose and also put across complex theological ideas in a way that everyone can understand. So what better way to see into another faith than through this oldest and most profound doorway – the doorway of story?

It has been my privilege and joy to sit and listen to these great stories as told by members of these faiths here in Britain today. I hope that, while putting them into simple words, I have managed to retain the sense of wonder and of awe which is so important to them – for these are stories for telling or for reading out aloud. The accompanying notes explain how the stories and festivals are celebrated now. I hope that many readers will wish to go on to see and share in these festivals with friends from the faiths.

The second part of the book takes us from the vast panorama of the great myths to the more intimate realm of the personal and family life-cycle. It is here, at birth or death for instance, that we can often hear most clearly the main beliefs of the faiths as they are simply told, and related to those aspects of life through which we all pass. Again, I hope that the descriptions of these family or community events will give some insight into their significance.

It has not been possible to cover all the faith communities that now make up our society. In particular, I have not been able to give adequate details of certain Christian communities, such as the Orthodox, Armenians, Copts, Polish or Ukrainian Catholics, and black Pentecostalists. (It is sometimes easy to forget that Christianity in Britain is as multi-cultural as any other faith.) Rather, I have tried to indicate a few of the windows into the lives and hopes, joys and beliefs of just some of the tremendous variety of faith communities in Britain today. That these windows have been opened for us is a great privilege, not to be taken lightly. So please remember, when you tell these stories or share in the events, that you are in the presence of the Divine, and walk quietly and with respect – for you walk on holy ground.

Martin Palmer

Acknowledgements

MY VERY SPECIAL THANKS to my friends from the faith communities for their invaluable help in supplying me with information and checking the final text to ensure its accuracy. In particular, Rabbi Douglas Charing, Mrs Padma Herat, Mr Loret Lee, the McCabe family, the monks and nuns of Manjushri Institute, Mr and Mrs Panchmatia, Habib ur Rahman, Ranchor das, Mr Salam, Mr Daljit Singh and Mrs Raj Kaur, Mrs Parnsri Wichagonrakul.

My gratitude also to the congregations of Bolton Hindu Temple, Cheetham Hill Mosque, Cheetham Hill Spanish and Portuguese Synagogue, Gandhi Hall Temple, Jackson's Row Synagogue, Sacred Trinity Church, Siri Guru Nanak Nirankari Gurdwara, the Thai Temple, the UK Islamic Mission, and the Manchester Chinese Education, Culture and Community Centre, who have welcomed me into their celebrations.

Finally, my deep appreciation of the help given by my former colleagues at Sacred Trinity Centre, especially Esther Bisset, Mike Edwards, Elizabeth Forde, Bob Hayfield, Jack Hogbin, Mary Ingrams and Mike Taylor.

Contents

Calendars

▲ *The Chinese calendar has a twelve-year cycle. Each year is named after an animal and this set of Chinese stamps shows the twelve animals.*

THE DIFFERENT RELIGIONS of the world use many calendars. Some are based on how long the earth takes to go round the sun. These are the solar calendars. Our Western calendar, with its 365 days and a leap year with an extra day every four years, is solar. Others are based on how long the moon takes to go round the earth – these are the lunar calendars. If you take twelve lunar months, which have 29 – 30 days each, and put them alongside the solar months with 28 – 31 days, you will see that the lunar year is 10 – 11 days shorter. Therefore, some lunar calendars have an extra month of 30 days every three years or so to bring them back into line with the solar year and the seasons. Below are brief descriptions of each major faith's calendar. (Faiths are listed alphabetically here and throughout the book.)

Buddhist: *Lunar.* Every three or four years there is an additional eighth month which brings the calendar back in line with the solar year. The twelve normal months are 29 – 30 days long.

Chinese: *Lunar.* The twelve normal months are 29 – 30 days long and every three or four years there is a 13th month. This enables the calendar to keep more or less in step with the solar year.

Christian: *Part lunar, part solar.* Christmas is a solar date – it is always December 25th in Britain. Easter is a lunar date and follows the Jewish lunar calendar. It can, therefore, be in very late March or any time in April.

Hindu and Sikh: *Most festivals are based on the lunar calendar, but a few, such as Baisakhi, are solar.* Every three years or so, the lunar calendar is brought back into line with the solar year by the addition of an extra month. The decision to add this month is only made in the preceding year and so the dates of Hindu and Sikh festivals cannot be determined more than a year in advance. The twelve normal months are 29 – 30 days long. They are divided into two sections of fifteen days each. The first fortnight after the new moon appears is called the dark fortnight; the second fortnight leading up to the full moon is called the light or bright fortnight.

Jewish: *Lunar.* Every three years an extra month is added to bring the calendar back in time with the solar year. The normal twelve months each have 29 – 30 days. Because of the extra month, festivals vary in their dates on the Western calendar. So Yom Kippur can be from early September to early October.

Muslim: *Lunar.* The Islamic calendar loses 10 – 11 days every year against the Western calendar, but no extra month is added so festivals move backwards every year. At present (1986) Eid ul-Fitr is in early June. In 1987 it will be in late May. In ten years' time it will be in early March. In about thirty-five years' time, it will have gone full circle and be back in June.

It is common in the West to use the Gregorian calendar which takes the number of the year from the supposed year of the birth of Jesus. So 1987 is seen as being the one thousand nine hundred and eighty seventh year after Jesus' birth. Dates are often called AD – from the Latin words *Anno Domini* – the Year of the Lord. Dates before Jesus are called BC – Before Christ – and run backwards. It is usual nowadays when writing for people of different faiths to use the terms 1987 CE – Common Era, or to talk of dates as BCE – Before Common Era.

The Chinese have a twelve-year cycle for their calendars, naming each year after one of twelve animals (see Chinese New Year, page 40).

There are a number of Hindu calendars which have different time spans. They differ from region to region.

The Jewish calendar is dated from the Creation of the World on the 1st of Tishri 3760 BCE. The letters AM appear after the date meaning *Anno Mundi* – Year of the World. 1986 is the year 5746 – 5747 AM.

For Muslims, the dates start from when Muhammad went to Medina, the Hijrah. So dates are labelled AH – After Hijrah. The Islamic year of 1407 AH runs from 5th September 1986 to 26th August 1987.

Festival Dates

THE FOLLOWING CALENDAR is designed to show roughly when the major festivals in the Buddhist, Chinese, Christian, Hindu, Jewish and Muslim religions take place. Details of the festivals of other faiths, such as the Bahai's, Jains and Parsis, can be found in the annual SHAP working party calendar of festivals (see page 86). It is impossible to give exact dates for all festivals for more than a year in advance because of the vast range of calendars and the very different means of calculating the dates of certain festivals.

Dates are given for festivals which remain constant. Where the festival falls within a certain limited period, say September to October, I have shown this. In the case of Islam, where the calendar is constantly moving backwards eleven or twelve days each year against the Western calendar, I have given the time span in which it will fall during 1984 – 1988. The festivals which are printed on a grey band are included in this book. Festivals which are not included in this book are described briefly.

January

1st   **Western New Year.** Largely secular, though Methodists hold a watch-night service to welcome the New Year.

6th   **Epiphany:** *Western Christian.*Celebrates the visit of the Wise Men to Jesus as a baby. Is the official end of Christmas (Twelfth Night).

6–7th   **Christmas:** *Orthodox Christian.*

18–19th   **Epiphany:** *Orthodox Christian.* Visit of the Wise Men to baby Jesus and also the baptism of Jesus.

January–February

    Chinese New Year.

February–March

Ash Wednesday: *Christian.* The start of Lent, a time of preparation for the events of Holy Week and Easter. A time of fasting and contemplation.

    Purim: *Jewish.*

Mahashivaratri: *Hindu.* Festival of the god Siva.

March–April

Palm Sunday and Holy Week: *Western Christian.* Palm Sunday celebrates Jesus' entry into Jerusalem, on a donkey. Holy Week celebrates the events of his last week before the crucifixion.

Christian pilgrims in Jerusalem on Palm Sunday. They carry palm leaves to recall the leaves thrown down in front of Jesus.

    Good Friday and Easter Sunday: *Western Christian.*

    Passover (Pesach): *Jewish.*

    Holi: *Hindu.*

Rama Naumi: *Hindu.*

Ching Ming: *Chinese.* Formal visits to the tombs of the ancestors are made and the sites cleared, food offered and the dead remembered.

At Ching Ming, Chinese families visit the tombs of their ancestors.

April

13th   **Baisakhi:** *Sikh.*

April–May

Easter: *Orthodox Christian.*

Lailat ul-Isra Wal Mi'raj. *Muslim.* Celebrates the prophet Muhammad's night journey by horse to Jerusalem and then up to Heaven.

Lailat ul-Bara'h: *Muslim.* The night of forgiveness, which comes as a preparation for Ramadan.

Ramadan (Eid ul-Fitr): *Muslim.*

May

Ascension Day: *Western Christian.* Celebrates Jesus going up into Heaven and his last earthly appearance to his disciples. Comes forty days after Easter.

May–June

Shavout: *Jewish.* Also known as Pentecost. Commemorates the giving of the Ten Commandments to Moses. It comes seven weeks after Pesach. It is also a harvest festival.

Whitsun (Pentecost): *Western Christian.*

Wesak: *Buddhist.*

Martyrdom of Guru Arjan Dev: *Sikh.*

Lailat ul-Qadr: *Muslim.*

Eid ul-Fitr: *Muslim.*

June

Dragon Boat: *Chinese.*

Ascension Day: *Orthodox Christian.* See above.

Whitsun (Pentecost): *Orthodox Christian.*

July

Dhammacakka: *Buddhist.*

July–August

Eid ul-Adha: *Muslim.*

August

Raksha Bandhan: *Hindu.* At this festival sisters give their brothers special bracelets of thread, called rakhis, which protect them.

At Raksha Bandhan, girls tie a colourful thread around their brothers' wrists – combining it with a flower or other decoration.

August–September

Day of Hijrah: *Muslim.* Start of Islamic new year. See calendar details on page 3.

Janmashtami: *Hindu.*

September

Moon Festival: *Chinese.*

September–October

Rosh Hashanah: *Jewish.*

Yom Kippur: *Jewish.*

Harvest Festival: *Christian.* Thanksgiving to God for the harvest.

Succot: *Jewish.* The feast of the Tabernacles which recalls the journeys of the people of Israel through the wilderness. In the synagogue and home gardens, temporary dwelling places (succot) are built out of branches and filled with fruit.

The Jewish festival of Succot is an agricultural festival. Here it is celebrated in school and children wave the lulav, a symbol made from palm branches, myrtle, willow and a lemon-like fruit – etrog.

October

Dusshera (Durga Puja or Navaratri): *Hindu.*

October–November

Divali: Hindu

Meelad ul-Nabi: *Muslim*. Celebration of prophet Muhammad's birthday.

Prayer is one of the Five Pillars of Islam and is, therefore, at the heart of every Muslim festival.

November

1st   **All Saints' Day:** *Christian*. The lives of the countless Christian saints and holy people are recalled and thanks is given for their example.

2nd   **All Souls' Day:** *Christian*. Traditional time to remember the dead and either pray for them or visit family graves.

Guru Nanak's Birthday: *Sikh*.

Martyrdom of Guru Tegh Bahadur: *Sikh*. The ninth Guru was martyred for the faith. Sikhs celebrate in a similar fashion to Guru Arjan Dev's Day.

Start of Advent: *Western Christian*. The first Sunday which is four Sundays away from Christmas Day. Time of preparation for Christmas.

November–December

Bodhi Day: *Buddhist*. The Mahayana celebration of the Enlightenment of the Buddha under the Bodhi tree. This is celebrated by Theravada Buddhists at Wesak.

December

Hanukkah (Chanucah): *Jewish*.

Birthday of Guru Gobind Singh: *Sikh*. Celebration of the tenth Guru founder of the Khalsa (see Baisakhi).

Reading the Guru Granth Sahib to celebrate a Sikh festival.

24th   **Christmas Eve:** *Western Christian*.

25th   **Christmas Day:** *Western Christian*.

Winter Festival: *Chinese*. Time of traditional feasts to build up strength to carry you through winter.

Baisakhi: Sikh

The story behind this festival tells how the great Sikh leader, Guru Gobind Rai, created the Khalsa, those who have dedicated their lives to God.

For many years the Sikhs had been hunted and killed – just because they loved God. Gobind Rai knew that he must try and stop this so he decided to test his followers. At a vast meeting in 1699 he stood before them, a sword in his hand, and called for a volunteer who would die for his faith. He then took the volunteer into a tent and reappeared, moments later, alone and with his sword dripping with blood. Again and again he called for volunteers, until five brave men had come forward. Each time the Guru reappeared alone, his sword covered in blood.

The crowd was very frightened when, suddenly, the Guru returned with all five men alive! To each of these courageous men he gave five things. As each of these things begins with the letter 'K' in Punjabi, they are known as the 'five Ks'. First he gave a kirpan – a sword to defend the good and the poor; next a bracelet to remind them of God's love (kara); then a command never to cut their hair (kesh); followed by a comb to keep it clean (kangha); finally a pair of shorts (kaccha) to help them when fighting.

But, most extraordinary of all, he changed everyone's surname. In India at that time, your surname labelled you as belonging to a particular caste or level of society and there was great prejudice between castes. The Guru did not like this because he knew God loves everyone equally. So he told all Sikhs to have either the name Singh (lion) if they were men, or Kaur (princess) if they were women. He changed his name from Gobind Rai to Gobind Singh. And, to this day, all Sikhs are still called Singh or Kaur.

When? Baisakhi is an old Indian festival, to which the Sikhs have given their own meaning. It falls on April 13th.

What happens? The festival lasts three days – two of which are spent continuously reading the Holy Book, the Guru Granth Sahib, in the temple. Five men take it in turns every two hours to read aloud until the entire book has been read. This takes until about 11.00 a.m. on the third day. Early on that day, new members of the Khalsa are admitted privately into the fellowship of the Khalsa. They drink a special amrit (sugar crystals in water) and receive the five Ks. The congregation gathers at the end of the reading for hymns, prayers, speeches and to share the fruit and karah parshad (ghee, milk, flour, sugar). Then they go on to the langar (free kitchen) for a vegetarian meal.

THE FOOD FOR THE FESTIVAL is karah parshad and fruit in the temple, then, either in the langar or at home, three or four vegetarian curries and special fried chapatis.

Why? Baisakhi marks the founding of the Khalsa, the start of strong Sikh self-identity. It stresses equality, love of God and care for all, regardless of colour, class or religion.

▶ *Guru Gobind Singh was the last of the human gurus of Sikhism. He founded the Khalsa – the brotherhood of Sikhism.*

◀ *A full-length kirpan or sword is traditionally worn by Sikhs – though some prefer to wear a small symbolic one like this. The kirpan is one of the 'five Ks' – the Sikh symbols.*

Christmas: Christian

When? Nobody really knows when Jesus was born. In many countries December 25th is celebrated as Christmas, but other countries celebrate January 6th or January 18th.

What happens? The festival in England starts in two ways. On Christmas Eve children hang up socks by their beds for Santa Claus, a mysterious Christian saint, to fill. Meanwhile, the churches are filled for the Midnight Mass to welcome the beginning of Christmas Day. In the morning, the children open their socks to find small presents. Larger presents are often laid out around the Christmas tree, a fir tree which is brightly decorated and covered with lights. After church in the morning, it will be time to open the presents and then the whole family will sit down to Christmas Dinner.

THERE ARE MANY traditional dishes at Christmas. Mince pies, shaped like cradles; Christmas pudding, a rich fruit pudding; a large roast bird. It is a time for rich and delicious food.

Why? Christians believe that Jesus was God – but that he was born like you and me so that he could speak to us and share our sort of life. Christmas is a time of rejoicing for his birth, and for friendship and children.

◀ *Shepherds come to visit the baby Jesus and the animals look on in wonder. For centuries the story of the Nativity has been a favourite subject for Christian artists.*

▶ *In December in schools all over the country, children act out the Christmas story. This Mary and Joseph take their parts very seriously.*

IN THE DAYS when the Romans ruled over Israel, the Emperor ordered a count of all his subjects. Everyone was told to return to their family town to be counted. So it was that a young man, Joseph, and his wife, Mary, arrived late one night in the town of Bethlehem, tired after a long journey. The town was packed with people and nowhere could they find a room. This was serious because Mary was about to have a baby and needed somewhere to rest. At last an innkeeper offered them his stable-cave and here the baby, Jesus, was born and placed in the animals' feeding trough, as a bed.

Jesus was no ordinary baby, and strange signs accompanied his birth. Angels appeared to shepherds sitting on a hill nearby, and told them to go to Bethlehem, to a stable to see a new king – a baby! They went, and there in the cave was the baby Jesus. A few days later, shortly after a new and very bright star had appeared in the sky, some wise men came to the stable. They were dressed like kings in rich clothes and they came to offer gifts to the baby before riding off again, back to the East.

It so happened that the king, Herod, heard of these wise men visiting Jesus and he was angry. He feared anyone who might be better than him, so he told his soldiers to kill all the babies in the country. But God warned Joseph and he took Mary and Jesus away to Egypt, before the soldiers could find them.

Dhammacakka:

Long ago in the land of India there lived a Prince called Siddhatha. The story of his life is told in the festival of Wesak (see page 50). For the festival of Dhammacakka the following tale is told.

WHEN THE PRINCE had left his comfortable home to wander through the world, he came into a forest. Here he met five monks who were living as simple a life as possible. They hoped that by living like this they would understand the world. The Prince joined them and tried to live a very simple life. At the end of six years, all he was eating was one grain of rice a day. But enlightenment had not come. So he gave up that path and wandered off to have a meal and to seek another path. His friends were disgusted with him.

Shortly afterwards he sat beneath the Bodhi tree and suddenly understood everything, thus becoming the Enlightened One, The Buddha. A few weeks later he met his five friends from the forest and preached his first great sermon to them in which he explained all that he now understood, and how this understanding would free people from the suffering of life. This first sermon is called 'The Setting in Motion of the Wheel of Truth' and is the basic teaching of Buddhism.

When? Dhammacakka day (Dhammacakka means Wheel of Truth) falls on the full moon day of the lunar month Asalaha, the day Buddha first preached. This is around July. (It is sometimes called Asalaha Puja day.)

What happens? Dhammacakka day comes immediately before Pansa, the Buddhist Lent. People visit the monasteries to listen to the monks teaching about the sermon and the Triple Gem – the Buddha, his teachings (Dhamma) and the community of monks (Sangha). Then everyone processes round the temple three times in honour of the Triple Gem. Gifts of food, usually curries, are brought to the monks. Other gifts include tall Pansa candles.

After Dhammacakka day, the Rainy Season, or Pansa starts. Monks may not stay away overnight, but should study and meditate in the monastery. Pansa lasts three months – the usual period of the rainy season.

FISH OR BEEF CURRIES are usually provided for the monks while other people eat spiced curries, quick fry dishes, 'Chinese' noodles, fish paste and rice.

Why? The teachings of the Buddha in his first sermon are the basic truths of Buddhism. Through the fellowship of monks, these teachings have been handed on. This is why Dhammacakka day is important.

▶ *This carving in stone from India shows the Buddha preaching his first sermon. On the right, wearing monks' robes, are the five hermits who he had lived with in the forest. They became his first five disciples. This event is remembered on Dhammacakka day.*

Buddhist

Divali: Hindu

When? Divali ('row of lights') starts on the thirteenth day of the dark fortnight of the month Ashwin (in October or November). It lasts three to five days and culminates in the day of Divali itself, usually on the third day, followed by New Year's Day.

What happens? About a week before Divali day itself, homes, shops and offices are cleaned and redecorated. In the forecourts and main halls, women trace elaborate designs using chalks and coloured flour – often using the arti-lamp as a basic design. In every window ghee lamps or candles are placed. On the 13th day of Ashwin, the goddess of fortune and wealth, Lakshmi (the wife of Vishnu) is worshipped. Her image and coins are washed with yoghurt and worshipped. Then on the 15th day, Divali itself, all account books have to be closed, all debts settled and every window brightly lit with lamps so Lakshmi can look in. Like Rama's return from exile, the past is tidied up – and a new start is made. It is a time to sort out disagreements and end quarrels with family and friends.

The next day is New Year. Fifty-six different kinds of food are cooked and piled up to resemble a mountain called Annakoot. The day closes with the burning of paper statues of evil Ravana.

Why? Divali is a very complicated festival, celebrated in many different ways – but the most important parts are the worship of Lakshmi for good and honest trade, the start of the New Year (hence the concern with closing the books) and the finishing of wicked Ravana.

◀ *This illustration from the Hindu Ramayana, the story of Rama, shows the monkeys building the bridge to Lanka.*

There are many stories told at Divali: of Krishna fighting the demon Narkasur and freeing the goddess Lakshmi, goddess of wealth; of Vishnu tricking King Bali. But the final and greatest story tells of King Rama and his return from exile.

Rama, with his consort Sita, ruled a great kingdom, but wicked people plotted against them and made them retreat out of the country into a forest. Here they lived quietly until, one fateful day, the fearful ten-headed demon king Ravana, swept down from the sky and carried off Sita to his palace on the island called Lanka (now Sri Lanka).

The monkey god, Hanuman, and Rama's brave brother, Lakshmana, helped King Rama to track Ravana down. With the help of the monkeys of India, a great bridge was built across to Lanka, over which poured the animal army of Rama. The battle swung to and fro, but at long last, using his magic bow, Rama killed the many-headed demon Ravana and rescued his beloved Sita. In triumph they returned to their kingdom, their exile now over.

▼ *At Divali, windows are brightly lit with lamps and Hindu women decorate the floors with beautiful patterns made from sand, chalks and coloured flour.*

Dragon Boat: Chinese

MANY YEARS AGO , there lived in China a good and honest official called Ch'u Yuen. He cared deeply for the people and always tried to help them. But the Emperor at that time was a wicked and greedy man. He wanted lots of money, so he made the ordinary people pay heavy taxes, until they were nearly starving.

When Ch'u Yuen saw this, he was very unhappy and decided he must do something. Now, in those days, any official who wanted to complain to the Emperor could write a special letter. By tradition the Emperor had to read such letters and pay attention to them. But when Ch'u Yuen wrote complaining about the poverty of the people, the Emperor laughed and threw the letter away.

Ch'u Yuen was heartbroken but decided that, in order to bring the Emperor to his senses, he must make the greatest sacrifice. He decided to kill himself.

Climbing to a cliff high above a lake, he threw himself into the lake and drowned. When the local people, who loved this man of justice, saw what was happening, they rushed to the lake – but were too late to save him. Suddenly the water around Ch'u Yuen's body began to churn, as up rose the evil dragons and demons intent upon eating the body. The villagers threw lumps of rice into the lake to divert the dragons and demons, while a boat sped out to pick up the body of noble Ch'u Yuen.

It is said that when the wicked Emperor heard the news, he was stricken with grief and changed his ways, giving back the money to the people.

▼ *Every year at the Dragon Boat festival, the boats with their carved dragon heads are raced against each other. The crews paddle furiously to the beat of a drum.* ▶

When? The Dragon Boat festival falls on the fifth day of the fifth month in the Chinese year – usually around early June.

What happens? Wherever possible, Chinese communities hold the great and lively 'Dragon Boat Race'. With beautiful light

boats, carved to resemble dragons, teams of rowers line up at the waterfront. Then, to the increasingly speedy beat of a drum, each team pulls away and races to a chosen spot in the water. And so the boat chase to save Ch'u Yuen's body is remembered.

RICE IS A SPECIALITY of this festival – glutinous rice made into dumplings like the lumps the villagers threw. These are wrapped in bamboo leaves and cooked in steam. It is also customary to eat salted duck eggs on this day.

Why? The honourable behaviour of Ch'u Yuen and the eventual victory of honour over evil, reflects many basic Taoist and Confucianist teachings. It is a celebration of justice, humanity and order – as well as of speed, water and summer.

When? Dusshera or Durga Puja or Navaratri (nine nights) is celebrated for ten days from the first night of Ashwin – which comes in September or October.

What happens? On each of the nights, different manifestations of the great goddess Devi are worshipped. Stories are told about the different forms she has taken and the heroic or noble deeds she has done. At the end of the festival, the statue of Durga – the warrior manifestation of Devi – is taken to a river, pool or to the sea and is lowered into the water to wash it. In some traditions, the first seven nights are fasting nights.

The great procession for the washing of the statue of Durga is a time for dancing and theatricals. It is also customary to give gifts at this time. This festival is one of the most popular and everyone joins in. In some places, the final night is when statues of Ravana, the devil king and enemy of Rama and Sita, are burned.

THE FESTIVAL has many great dishes of fruit curries and nuts. But it is also a time for fasting.

Why? Devi is the most important female deity. As such she represents power, war, love, com-

Dusshera: Hindu

The great goddess Devi has many names and many stories told about her. As Kali she destroys Kal (time). As Parvati she is a faithful wife to her husband, Siva, and mother to her children, Ganesha and Kartikeya. But it is as Durga, riding on her lion, that she is best known. And her battle with evil Mahisha is a great tale.

THE GODDESS DURGA had come with her army to slay the buffalo demon, Mahisha, and his terrible army. Her troops destroyed Mahisha's soldiers. This roused the buffalo demon to dreadful anger. Lashing out with his hooves, piercing with his horns and whipping with his tail, he thundered towards Durga, slaying her troops. The earth shook, the waters foamed at this struggle. Mahisha tried to attack Durga's lion mount. Durga lassooed him, but he changed into a lion and escaped. Durga cut off his head, but he became a man. She shot him with arrows, but he became a great elephant. She cut off his trunk and he became a buffalo again. Durga leapt onto his neck and, with her trident spear, struck him dead. At his death, all good creation cheered – while the forces of evil ran away in confusion.

▲ *Durga, mounted on her lion, battles with the buffalo demon.*

▶ *In some parts of India, huge models of the ten-headed demon king, Ravana, are built at Dusshera.*

passion, beauty, terror, death and energy. Everyone can find one or more of her manifestations which appeals to them, so her festival is very popular.

When? In Western churches, Easter, the day Jesus rose from the dead, comes on the first Sunday after the spring full moon. In Eastern churches, it falls anything up to five weeks later. Western Easter occurs in March or April and Eastern Easter in April or May.

What happens? Palm Sunday comes a week before Easter Sunday and commemorates Jesus coming into Jerusalem. Palm leaves and crosses are given out because the crowds waved these to welcome him. The week from Palm Sunday onwards is Holy Week, and Christians pray and study the story of Jesus' dramatic last week. On Maundy Thursday, the special meal – the Communion – which Jesus shared with his friends, is celebrated, often with a simple meal in church. Good Friday is a day of prayer and meditation as Christians join in the three-hour service which ends at 3.00 p.m., the time of Jesus' death. But it is Easter Sunday which is most glorious, for then Christians celebrate Jesus' victory over death and his resurrection. The churches are full of flowers, and Easter eggs are given to children to show new life.

THE EASTER EGG, either hard-boiled with a painted or decorated shell, or made of chocolate, is an important part of Easter celebrations. On Good Friday, small buns marked with a cross and called hot cross buns are eaten.

Easter: Christian

IT WAS IN PALESTINE that it all happened. Jesus came, preaching and healing, telling people to love God and to prepare for his Kingdom. The Roman and Jewish authorities watched with growing fear as Jesus came down to Jerusalem. When the crowds all rushed out to meet him, the rulers knew he must be got rid of, but how? He was always surrounded by loving crowds.

One night, a follower of Jesus, called Judas, came to the leaders and offered to tell them when and where to capture Jesus. So, one Thursday night, after a special meal with his friends, Jesus was arrested while praying in a quiet garden.

He was taken to prison, whipped, spat at and a crown of thorn branches was pushed on his head. In the morning he was condemned to die by being crucified.

On a hill outside the city, Jesus' hands and feet were nailed to a cross, the cross was raised and he was left to die. At midday the sky turned black and the earth shook and at three in the afternoon he died.

He was taken down and buried in a cave-tomb by his friends. Rolling a great stone to cover the door they left sadly.

But God raised Jesus from the dead and, when his friends returned to the tomb, it was empty. Then Jesus came to his friends to show that God can defeat even death. And his friends set off into the world to tell others of God's love.

▲ *In a Good Friday street theatre, Roman soldiers lead Jesus to his crucifixion.*

▶ *In some countries, Easter eggs are beautifully patterned with wax and dyes.*

Why? Christians believe Jesus showed that life does not end at death, but that, if they love Jesus and act according to his teaching and recognise their failings, then God will give them new life after death.

Eid ul-Adha: Muslim

Way back in the earliest times, there lived a great prophet called Abraham, who knew and believed in the One God, Allah. Abraham had a son, Isma'ail, of whom he was very fond. Isma'ail was a quiet and helpful boy, who also loved Allah. But one day Abraham had a strange and frightening dream. In his dream, he was commanded to take Isma'ail and sacrifice him as an offering to Allah. With great sadness Abraham went and told his son all he had dreamt. Without a moment's hesitation, Isma'ail replied that, if this was what Allah wanted, then they must do it.

So Isma'ail lay down and Abraham, a sharp knife in his hand, prepared to do what Allah commanded. He was just about to sacrifice Isma'ail when the voice of Allah spoke, telling him not to harm the boy. Amazed and delighted, Abraham and Isma'ail realized that the dream had been a test – to see how much they really loved and trusted Allah. Then Abraham found that Allah had placed an animal, some say a ram, others a goat, nearby. This he killed in place of Isma'ail. Now this great and fearful test took place on a large rock, set on a hill. This hill later became the city of Mina and the site of this story is said to be under the great mosque in Mina. Pilgrims on Hajj (see below) visit the site every year.

When? Eid ul-Adha (Festival of Sacrifice) falls in the 12th month of the Islamic year, at the end of the time called Hajj. At this time many Muslims go on pilgrimage (Hajj) to the Holy City of Mecca. This festival at present falls in July or August.

What happens? Wearing new clothes, the whole family will be up before dawn to get to the mosque for the dawn prayer. Then the day is in full swing. The sacrifice of a lamb or sheep takes place. The animals must be killed as swiftly as possible with one knife cut, and they must have their heads towards Mecca. Sections from the Holy Book, the Qur'an, are read while the sacrifice takes place. The meat is then shared, not just amongst the family but, more importantly, with the poor and with neighbours. Eid cards and gifts are given and children get special attention.

Lamb is, of course, the main food eaten at this festival. It is often roasted whole with a piece of confectionary in its mouth and is served with a wide range of dishes and sauces.

Why? 'Islam' is often translated as 'submission' to the will of Allah. The story of Abraham and Isma'ail is a powerful reminder of how Allah provides and cares for those who do his will.

▶ *Eid ul-Adha celebrates the end of the time of Hajj – pilgrimage to Mecca. Here pilgrims walk around the Ka'ba and kiss the black stone in the Ka'ba wall.*

◀ *At Eid ul-Adha, Muslim shops will be full of Eid cards.*

When? The festival of Eid ul-Fitr, breaking the fast of Ramadan, comes when the new moon is sighted at the end of Ramadan. At present this is in May or June.

What happens? During Ramadan, Muslims, unless they are travellers, children under ten, pregnant or sick, fast from sunrise to sunset. The fast is usually ended by first eating a date. New clothes are worn and Eid cards and gifts sent. The day starts with dawn prayer at the mosque. After

this, the families give generously to charity. (This is called Zakat ul-Fitr.) This offering must be food or money and is one of the five duties of all Muslims. After the zakat, comes the festival prayer; families will go, if possible, to the cemetery to pray for the dead and to remember that they, too, will die one day. After a good breakfast – the first proper one for thirty days – the families go out to give each other the Eid greeting – 'Eid Mubarak' (blessed festival).

SWEETS are a major treat at this festival; particularly attractive boxes of sugared almonds, laid out in patterns.

Why? The foundation of Islam stems from the Qur'an which the Angel Gabriel dictated to Muhammad (see page 35). It is not surprising that Muhammad had a difficult and often dangerous time, and Muslims have to learn to control themselves and to put Allah before all else. Ramadan helps in this, while Eid ul-

24

Eid ul-Fitr: Muslim

IN THE DAYS when the prophet Muhammad lived, the great cities of Mecca and Medina were still places where false gods were worshipped. Only slowly was the Prophet able to call people away from their false gods, to knowledge of the One God, Allah.

So, when Muhammad came to the citizens of Mecca, telling them of all that the Angel Gabriel had told him, he found few people who believed him and many who opposed him. Soon it became impossible for the Prophet to stay in Mecca. At just the right time, a letter came from believers in the city of Medina, inviting the Prophet to come to them.

When he arrived, he found a divided and feuding city. He set to and brought order to the city. As the people began to grow used to the Muslim way of life, the Prophet abolished all the many pagan festivals and gave all Muslims two major festivals instead. One was Eid ul-Adha (see page 22); the other was Eid ul-Fitr. Furthermore, he established a time of fasting and of self-restraint – called Ramadan. The Prophet decreed that this fast should last thirty days, and its end was to be the joyful celebration of Eid ul-Fitr. And so it is to this day.

▲ *Eid ul-Fitr, like all Muslim festivals, is a time for prayer. Here Muslims pray in the mosque. Then they will go to the cemetery to pray for the dead.*

▶ *Eid ul-Fitr is another occasion for Muslims to send Eid cards to their friends with the greeting 'Eid Mubarak'*

Fitr celebrates the glory and triumph of Allah, but also stresses, through zakat, the responsibilities of being a Muslim.

Eid Mubarak

When? Guru Nanak's birthday is celebrated on the full moon day of November.

What happens? The festival starts two days before full moon, with a continuous reading by a team of readers of the Holy Book, the Guru Granth Sahib, in the gurdwara (temple). When this finishes on the morning of the full moon, the usual act of worship takes place. After this, and throughout the rest of the day, stories about Guru Nanak, his experiences, teachings and the opposition he encountered, are told. There are often speeches as well. Throughout the day the langar (free kitchen) supplies food, given by families coming to the gurdwara. Some people will also mark the occasion with a night-long fast.

NO MEAT is eaten during festivals, just lots of curried vegetables like aubergines, cabbage, lady's fingers – and chapatis, which are fried.

Why? The teachings of Guru

▲ *Guru Nanak was one of the first to teach the Sikh religion. He is shown sitting under the bel tree – the traditional Indian tree of wisdom (also called the Bodhi tree). His disciples are gathered round him.*

Nanak mark the first steps in the formation of the Sikh religion. His way of life also acts as a model for Sikhs to follow. In celebrating his birth, the community remembers his example and rejoices in his teachings.

Birthday: Sikh

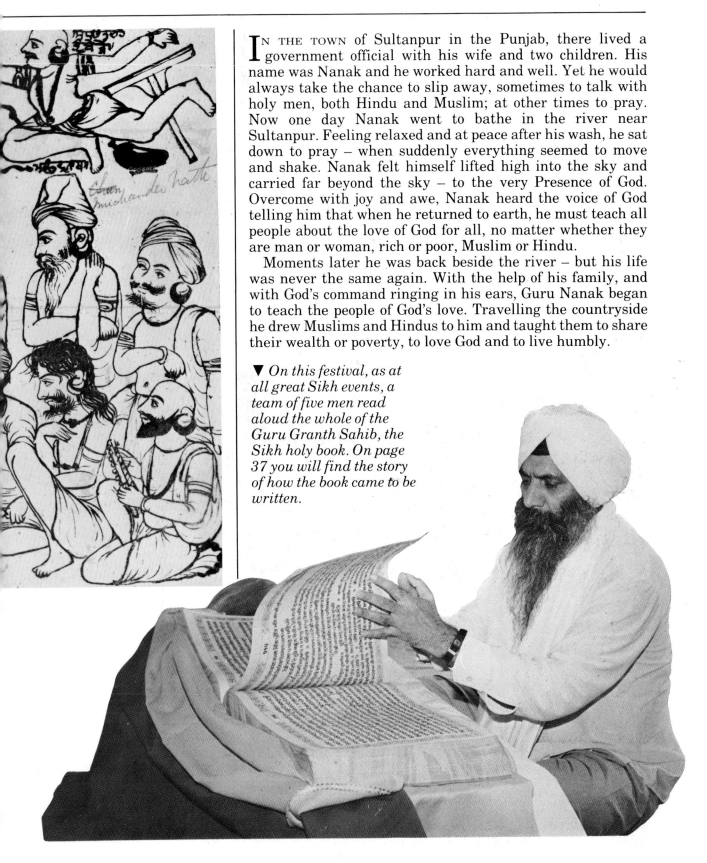

IN THE TOWN of Sultanpur in the Punjab, there lived a government official with his wife and two children. His name was Nanak and he worked hard and well. Yet he would always take the chance to slip away, sometimes to talk with holy men, both Hindu and Muslim; at other times to pray. Now one day Nanak went to bathe in the river near Sultanpur. Feeling relaxed and at peace after his wash, he sat down to pray – when suddenly everything seemed to move and shake. Nanak felt himself lifted high into the sky and carried far beyond the sky – to the very Presence of God. Overcome with joy and awe, Nanak heard the voice of God telling him that when he returned to earth, he must teach all people about the love of God for all, no matter whether they are man or woman, rich or poor, Muslim or Hindu.

Moments later he was back beside the river – but his life was never the same again. With the help of his family, and with God's command ringing in his ears, Guru Nanak began to teach the people of God's love. Travelling the countryside he drew Muslims and Hindus to him and taught them to share their wealth or poverty, to love God and to live humbly.

▼ *On this festival, as at all great Sikh events, a team of five men read aloud the whole of the Guru Granth Sahib, the Sikh holy book. On page 37 you will find the story of how the book came to be written.*

Hanukkah: Jewish

AT LONG LAST, after years of bitter, bloody fighting, the Jewish people were free. The armies of the vile Seleucid Emperor had been thrown out and, best of all, Jerusalem with its temple was in Jewish hands again.

But what a sight greeted the Jews at the temple. This most sacred place had been wickedly misused by the Seleucids, who did not believe in the One God and had put many statues there. They had also sacrificed pigs in the Holy of Holies – a most terrible thing to do.

Now the temple had to be restored and first of all the Menorah, the sacred light reminding Jews of God's presence, had to be relit. Hunting around amongst the filth left by the Seleucid soldiers, Judah Maccabee, leader of the Jewish fighters, found a small pot of oil – just enough for one day. It was going to take eight days to make new olive oil for the lamp, but Judah decided to use up the little pot because, even though it wouldn't last, it would show that all was now well. So the great Menorah, the seven-branched candlestick was lit. But, wonder of wonders, the oil lasted not one day, not two, but eight days, giving enough time for the new oil to be made. So the light never went out. Truly God was with them.

▲ *The Hanukkah candlestick is based on the Menorah – the great seven-branched candlestick – which was kept in the Temple at Jerusalem. In 70 CE the Romans destroyed the temple. In this carving you can see the Roman soldiers carrying away the Menorah.*

◀ *Lighting the Hanukkah candles – here, on the fourth day of the festival, four candles are lit with the 'servant candle'.*

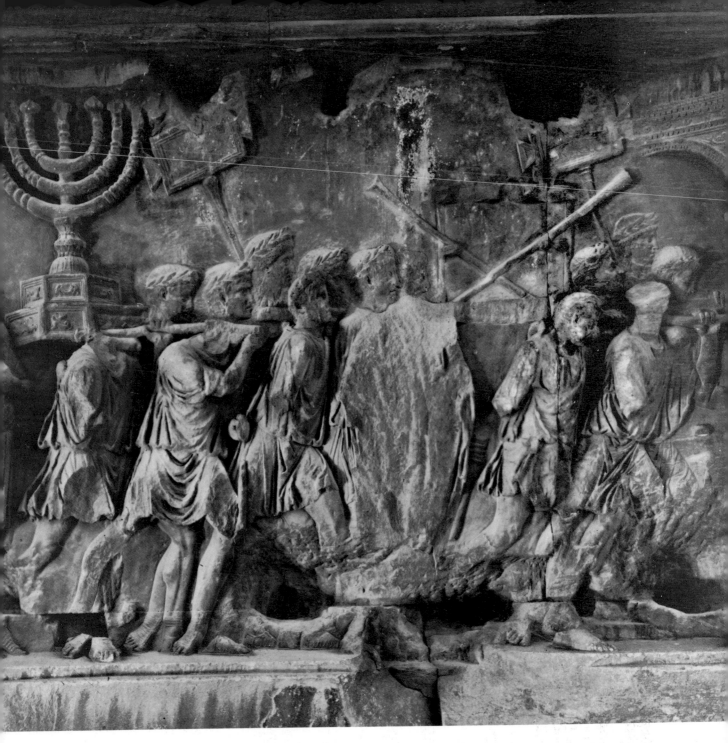

When? Hanukkah starts on the 25th of the month of Kislev, which usually places it around December.

What happens? The central focus of each of the eight days of the festival is the lighting of the Hanukkah candles. The normal seven-branched candlestick is replaced by one with eight*, to

*Sometimes there are nine candle holders – one to hold the 'servant' candle which is used to light the other eight candles.

commemorate the eight days the oil lasted. Each evening before a new day, a candle is lit, until, on the eighth day, all the candles are alight. During the festival, parties are held where a special game is spinning the dreidle. This small top has Hebrew letters on each edge. Depending on which letter it ends up on, you can either take from the 'bank' of sweets or nuts, etc, or you have to put in. This game has led to a general development of parties and party games at this time.

FOOD COOKED IN OIL is traditional at Hanukkah because of the oil of the temple. For instance, latkes or levivot which are pancakes made from potatoes and fried in oil.

Why? History has dealt some cruel and harsh blows to the Jewish people, but they have always known that God is with them. In the story of Hanukkah, both the suffering and survival are emphasised, plus the symbol of God's presence.

Holi: Hindu

When? Holi, the festival of love, comes on the full moon day of the month Falgun – March to April.

What happens? On the eve of Holi, children often act the story of how Vishnu killed the demon Hiranya Kashipa. Vishnu appeared as the man-lion, Narasimha, to save his devotee Prahlad. The name Holi comes from the demon goddess Holika who tried to kill Prahlad by burning him on her lap. But Vishnu burnt her to death. Prahlad was sorry for her and promised to name a festival for her, Holi. On the eve of Holi, huge bonfires are lit and grain is cooked along with coconuts, to celebrate harvest and the earth's fertility.

The next day, beware! People take to the streets to throw coloured water at each other. Legend has it Krishna played this trick on the cowmaids. It is a time for fun, tricks and dancing and everyone joins in. In many regions there are other special events at Holi.

FOOD AT THIS FESTIVAL includes grain and coconuts to celebrate the fertility of the earth. These

IN BYGONE DAYS, the great god Vishnu decided to kill the demon king Kansa. He came to this world as a baby, and was saved from the wicked Kansa by being taken to a peasant's house (see Janmashtami, page 32). Here, as the child Krishna, he grew up.

But Kansa sought to destroy him and sent a demon woman called Putana. She roamed the countryside giving poisoned milk from her breast to every baby she saw. Krishna, however, knew her evil ways and killed her instead.

By the time Krishna was a young man, he was full of tricks. One day he saw some cowmaids swimming in a pond. Very quietly he crept up and stole their clothes. To get them back, the maids had to come out one by one, bow before Krishna and then he returned their clothes. So beautiful was he that they all fell in love with him and they all wanted to dance with him. By use of his great powers, Krishna was able to make all the maids think he had danced with them when, really, they had all danced in one great circle. Perhaps the god of pleasure, Kama, (whose bow of love is a sugarcane, with a line of humming bees for a string and flowers for arrows) had been at work – for in this dance Krishna met his true love, the maid Radha.

are roasted in the bonfires and eaten.

Why? The harvest is a time to think of the fruitfulness of the land. It is also a time of thinking about love and this is why there are teasing and games in honour of Krishna, the divine lover.

▶ At Holi, the teasing game which Krishna played on the cow girls is remembered – he stole their clothes while they were bathing.

▼ In some places, people throw coloured water at each other at Holi.

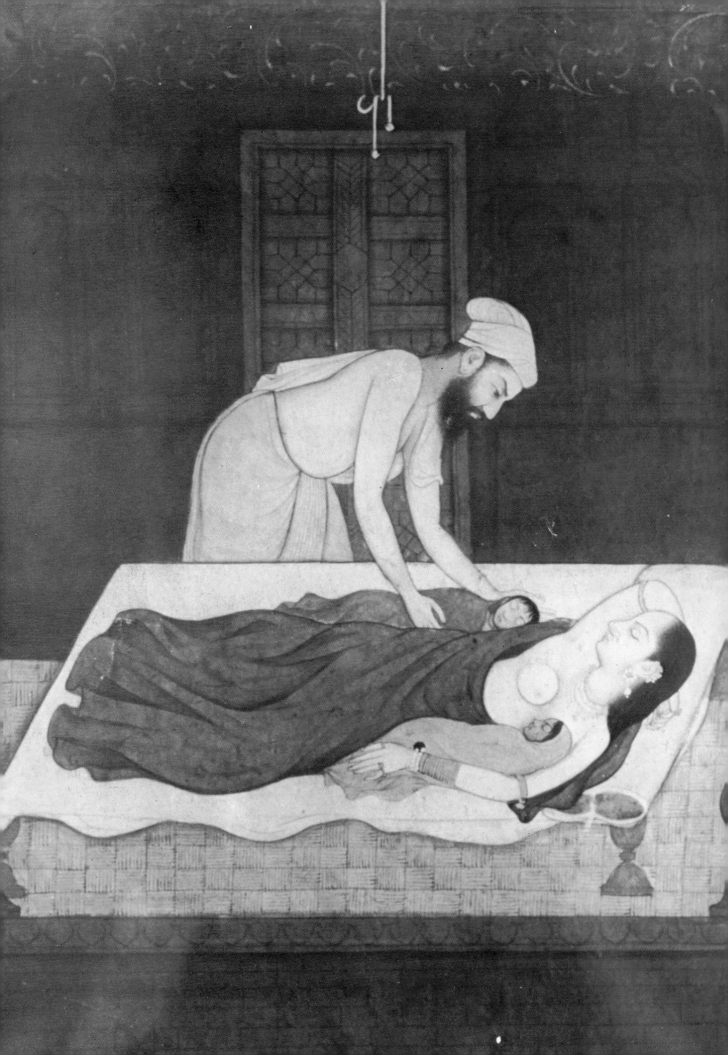

Janmashtami: Hindu

When? Janmashtami, Krishna's birthday, falls on the eighth day of Shravan – which comes between July and September.

What happens? The real celebration starts at midnight – the time of Krishna's birth. All that day people do not eat but instead come to the temple to watch their children acting stories about Krishna. When there is no acting, the older people tell stories of Krishna. Just before midnight a statue of the baby Krishna is washed with yoghurt, ghee, honey, sugar and milk.

The mixture is collected and shared out as a special drink for everyone. Then the statue or a picture of Krishna is put on a little decorated swing which everyone is allowed to push, to entertain the baby. At midnight the arti ceremony is performed with the lamp and then a huge feast is held.

YOGHURT, milk and honey are used to make a wide range of dishes and sweets. No meat or grain is eaten.

Why? Krishna is believed to be one of the most important representations or incarnations (avatars) of the great god Vishnu. He not only fights evil but also enjoys and loves life itself. So his birth is a time of happiness and fun as the old stories of good, evil and laughter are told.

◀ *Devaki's husband takes the baby Krishna to safety. Another baby is left behind to trick the evil Kansa.*

▶ *A picture of Krishna sits among the decorations on the swing that Hindus build at Janmashtami. Everyone has a turn at pushing the swing to amuse the baby Krishna.*

THERE ONCE DWELT on earth a terrible demon called Kansa. He was evil and cruel and ruled the world. One day he heard a voice from Heaven telling him that his sister, Devaki, would have a child who would kill him. Frightened and angry, he seized his sister and her husband and locked them in a deep dungeon. Six children were born and Kansa killed them all.

The great god Vishnu decided to rid the world of evil Kansa and chose to come to earth as a baby, called Krishna. So it was that Devaki became pregnant again and the baby Krishna grew within her.

To protect Krishna from the demon Kansa, the gods planned to trick him. When Krishna was born, the soldiers on guard fell fast asleep. Devaki's husband then hurried out of the dungeon and took the baby across the river Jamuna to live with a herdsman, far outside the city. The gods then put a special girl baby in the cradle. When the soldiers awoke, they rushed off to tell Kansa of the new baby. He came and picked up the child to kill her. But, suddenly, the baby flew into the air, for she was a goddess, and laughing aloud she told Kansa that Krishna was alive and well and would return to kill him.

Kansa searched the world high and low, but he never caught Krishna, who grew up waiting his time.

Lailat ul-Qadr: Muslim

When? Lailat ul-Qadr, the night of power, comes on the 27th day of Ramadan – at present it falls in May to June.

What happens? It is a festival of the night, and so the main events take place at night time. After the final prayers of the day, following sunset, the Ramadan fast is broken and then, through the night until the dawn prayer, the Qur'an will be read aloud in the mosque. It is also a time for quiet prayer, and for asking for forgiveness. Some people will also visit the cemetery, if possible, to remember the dead.

AS THE FESTIVAL FALLS at the end of Ramadan, the month of fasting, there are no special feasts. Rather it is a time of abstinence and of reflection.

Why? Muslims believe Muhammad was the final prophet and that, through him, God revealed once and for all his will. The Qur'an is that revelation and it lies at the centre of Islam. Hence the importance of celebrating the night it was first revealed.

◀ *The gift of the Qur'an, the final revelation of Allah, is celebrated at Lailat ul-Qadr.*

▶ *During Ramadan, Muslims fast all day. Then, after sunset, they have a simple meal, often beginning with dates. Before they eat, they give thanks to Allah for their food. Ramadan lasts for 30 days and Lailat ul-Qadr falls on the 27th day.*

IN DAYS GONE BY, there lived in the rich but pagan city of Mecca, a man called Muhammad. He worked hard and was honest and everyone trusted him. But at heart he was worried. All around him he saw false gods being worshipped. So he used to go up into the hills nearby, to a special cave, where he prayed and meditated.

One night when Muhammad was 40 years old, he was in the cave when a voice spoke, asking him to read. Terrified, he stayed silent. But the voice spoke again and yet again. At last Muhammad stammered, 'I cannot read'. Then the voice asked him to repeat the following words:

Proclaim, In the name of the Lord and cherisher,
Who created man out of a clot of congealed blood:
Proclaim, and thy Lord is most bountiful,
He who taught how to use the pen,
Taught man that which he did not know.

Then the voice revealed itself as the Angel Gabriel, sent from God to give the world the Qur'an. Muhammad was to be the pen which wrote down for all to read, the words of God. Thus were the first words given on that night.

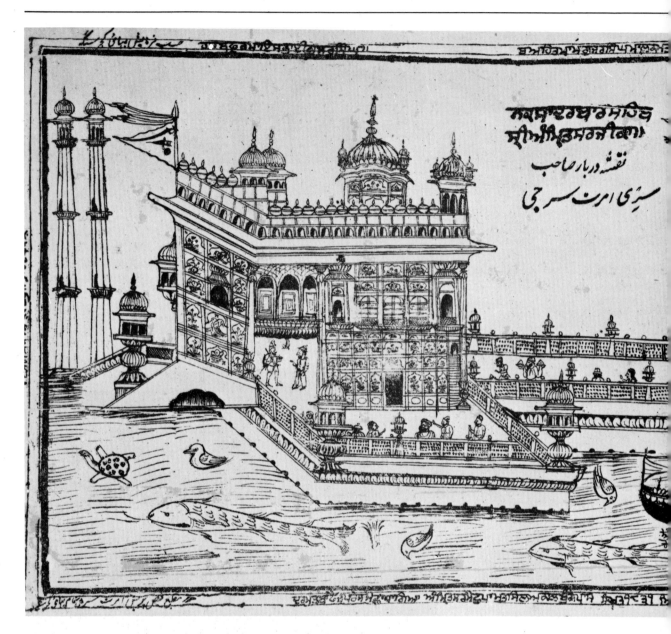

▲ *The Golden Temple at Amritsar in India is the centre of Sikhism. This old picture shows fish and birds in the pool, or tank, which surrounds the temple. The water of the temple is believed to be very holy, like amrit, the sacred drink of the Sikhs – and that is why the city is called Amritsar.*

When? The martyrdom of Guru Arjan Dev is recalled in the early summer – between May and June.

What happens? The festival is a lively and celebratory one and lasts three days. The first two are spent reading the Guru Granth Sahib, the Sikh Holy Book, in the gurdwara (temple). When the reading finishes on the third day, the usual service takes place, but with special hymns and speeches. Then the congregation go to the free kitchen, the langar, for a festival meal.

THE NORMAL festival foods are cooked. Shabil, a mixture of milk, sugar and water (similar to a milk shake) is made and drunk throughout the day with other soft drinks.

Guru Arjan Dev: Sikh

THE TEACHINGS of the Sikh Gurus were spreading throughout India. Many people were turning to these teachings because they were more gentle than those of the invading Muslims. They taught of the One God and no others and so differed from Hinduism.

Now Guru Arjan Dev was teacher of the Sikhs and he was worried. Jealous men were plotting against the Sikhs and he feared for his friends. How could he help to hold them together? After praying and meditating, he decided on two ways. First, he would build a glorious temple to God, a special place for Sikhs wherever they were. So he ordered the Golden Temple of Amritsar to be built – it still stands today. Secondly, he had the teachings of the Gurus written down, the hymns and prayers. To this he added some of the beautiful words in other faiths. Within a remarkably short time, he had finished and the Holy Book, some 1430 pages long, was ready. The Adi Granth (later called the Guru Granth Sahib) was to be of enormous help to the Sikhs in the difficult and dangerous years ahead.

The Muslim leaders grew more and more jealous of the Sikhs and so it was that, one day, Guru Arjan was seized and imprisoned. When he refused to give up his beliefs, he was cruelly and terribly tortured until, in great pain, he died – the first Sikh martyr.

Why? The Guru Granth Sahib is the Holy Book. Therefore it is natural to celebrate its compiler. But also, on this day, Sikhs remember their freedom and how it was won by the martyrs.

▶ *The Golden Temple as it is today – reflected in the holy water around it. Sikhs from around the world come to their beautiful temple at Amritsar.*

Moon Festival: Chinese

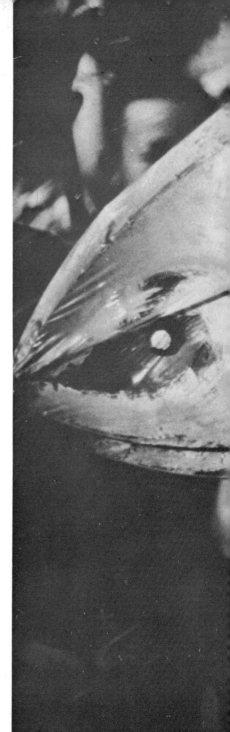

IN DAYS OF OLD, there lived a wicked king in China. Although he was terrible, his wife Sheung Ngao was a kind and loving woman who was sad at the evil her husband did.

One day this king heard of a magic potion which would cause anyone who drank it to live for ever. He commanded his servants to search the world for the magic potion and to bring it to him.

After many adventures, the crew of one of his ships found the magic potion and brought it home. The king put the potion in his room and announced that, on the following day, he would drink it and thus live for ever. The people were very sorry to hear this, because he was so wicked.

That night his wife, Sheung Ngao, sat up wondering. If the king lived for ever, she knew that his people would suffer for ever. So she decided to do one last act of kindness, knowing her husband would surely kill her afterwards. She stole into his room and drank the magic potion. When the king found out, he rushed to kill brave Sheung Ngao – but the gods lifted her from his grasp and carried her to the moon, where she lives to this day.

▲ At the autumn Moon Festival Chinese children see who can make or buy the most interesting lantern.

◄ Moon cakes are an important part of this festival. They have various things inside: lotus or melon or egg. They are all very filling!

When? The brightest full moon occurs on the fifteenth day of the

eighth lunar month and, because it falls in September, it is also known as the mid-autumn festival or lantern festival.

What happens? For days before the festival, food and lanterns are prepared. The lanterns, of all shapes, sizes and colours, some like fish, others in various animal shapes, form the highlight of the festival. When darkness comes, the bright moon is greeted with burning incense sticks and with a beautiful procession of lanterns. People look to see Sheung Ngao on the moon, and feast together. It is a time for family reunions as well as a traditional time for weddings to be arranged and engagements announced.

MOON CAKES are an important part of this festival. Various fillings (lotus or melon or egg are the most common) are baked in pastry cases. With the cakes go peanuts and boiled taro roots as well as many fruits.

Why? Autumn is always an important time for agriculture and the bright moon gives a good opportunity for celebration. The moon cakes were once used to hide messages in when the Chinese revolted and threw out the Mongolians. So they are a reminder of Chinese patriotism — as well as representing the fullness and bounty of the autumn moon.

New Year: Chinese

When? Chinese New Year is the first day of the first month of the lunar calendar. It falls between late January and mid February.

What happens? In the days before New Year, homes are swept and cleaned and all sharp knives are put away. To sweep on New Year might mean you pushed good luck out. In each kitchen, the paper picture of the kitchen god watches over the family all year. On New Year's Eve, he returns to heaven to report on the family's behaviour. Before the paper is burnt, offerings are made, especially sweet ones so he will say sweet things.

New Year's Day arrives with noise. Fireworks explode, drums beat and cymbals clang as the lion dance goes through the streets. Led by a boy dressed as the future happy Buddha, the lion dances from house to house, collecting the lucky money bags and vegetables which hang outside for him. This brings good luck to the shop or house. The air fills with cries of 'Kung Hei Fat Choy' – Happy New Year. Many families have a flowering bush in the house, cultivated to flower on New Year.

CHILDREN RECEIVE lucky money bags (small red envelopes) and a great feast is prepared – but with no meat, as a sign of respect to animals. Oranges and tangerines – symbols of long life – accompany the vegetable dishes. A special nut-filled pastry shaped like a small conch shell is particularly popular.

Why? New Year is always an alarming and exciting time. The celebration with its noise scares away the evil of the past and prepares, through lucky symbols and deeds, to greet the New Year, which may be good.

So LONG AGO no one can really remember when, there was a king in China who wished to celebrate the New Year in style. He decided not only to invite the people but also the animals in his kingdom to a feast. So he sent out messengers to all his people and to all the animals that dwelt in the land.

The great day came and the hall was filled with food and drink. The king awaited his animal guests.

First to arrive were Rat and Ox. They settled down after greeting the king. Next came Tiger, Hare and Dragon and they filled the hall with colour and splendour. Following them came Snake, Horse and Ram who greeted the king and took their seats. After them, in bounced Monkey with Cock and Dog close behind. Finally, Pig strolled in and took his place. The king waited. But no more animals came. He was angry and sad that this was so, and decided to thank those animals which had come, in a very special way. Thus he decreed that each year would have the name of one of the animals, starting with Rat and ending with Pig. At the end of twelve years (the number of animals that had come) the cycle would start again with Rat. And so it is to this day.

▲ At Chinese New Year, children are given 'red packets' which contain money. This is to bring good luck and wealth. Another sign of good luck is if the New Year tree blossoms at this time.

▶ The New Year brings the Lion Dance. Houses and shops are decorated with vegetables and red money packets and, when the lion dances by and takes these, it brings good luck.

Passover: Jewish

ONG AGO the Jews lived as slaves in Egypt. Their life was hard and cruel. The Pharoah so hated and feared them that he ordered all the Jewish baby boys to be killed. One child escaped. His mother hid him by the river where an Egyptian princess found him and brought him up. His name was Moses.

Moses saw the suffering of his people and was angry. Now God spoke to Moses and told him to go to Pharoah and ask that his people be set free. God promised all would be well. So Moses came to Pharoah, but Pharoah refused and made the people work even harder.

Then God caused strange things to happen. The river Nile turned to blood, frogs swarmed over the land, wild animals and insects came forth, boils appeared on people and so on. But still Pharoah refused to let the Jews go. Finally God told Moses that he was going to kill the eldest boy in each house – but the Jewish families would be saved if they killed a lamb and put its blood on their door posts. Then the Angel of Death would pass by. And so the Egyptians lost their eldest sons but the Jewish sons survived.

Pharoah had now had enough. He ordered the Jews to go at once. Moses gathered his people together – they only had enough time to eat the lamb they had killed and to make flat bread before setting off. Thus the Jews were on their way home, but many troubles still lay before them.

When? Passover (Pesach) lasts eight days, and starts on the 15th day of the month Nisan – between March and April.

What happens? Because the Jews did not have time to let the bread rise before they left Egypt, no leavened bread is permitted during the festival. Before the festival begins, all mixtures of flour and water are cleared out and the house is thoroughly cleaned. An unleavened bread, called matzah, is made or bought.

The main event is Seder night. The family gather in the home and the evening starts with the retelling of the Exodus story. The main parts of the story are highlighted by the youngest child asking questions and by the symbols found at the meal. Four glasses of wine are drunk to remember the four acts of salvation (outlined in Exodus 6: 6-7). The wine is also spilt at the mention of each plague to show sorrow for those necessary but hurtful acts. Matzah is eaten to remember how swiftly the Jews left Egypt. Bitter herbs – horseradish – evoke the bitterness of slavery. Vegetables dipped in salt water recall the tears shed in oppression. Also on the Seder plate are a shankbone to recall the lamb, and an egg to recall the festival offering.

Many other traditions have grown up, such as leaving a full glass for Elijah, should he return.

OTHER FESTIVAL FOODS such as sweet cakes or special dishes associated with certain places where the Jews live outside Israel (in Diaspora), are eaten.

Why? The great act of liberation showed the Jews that God was their God, and they were his chosen people.

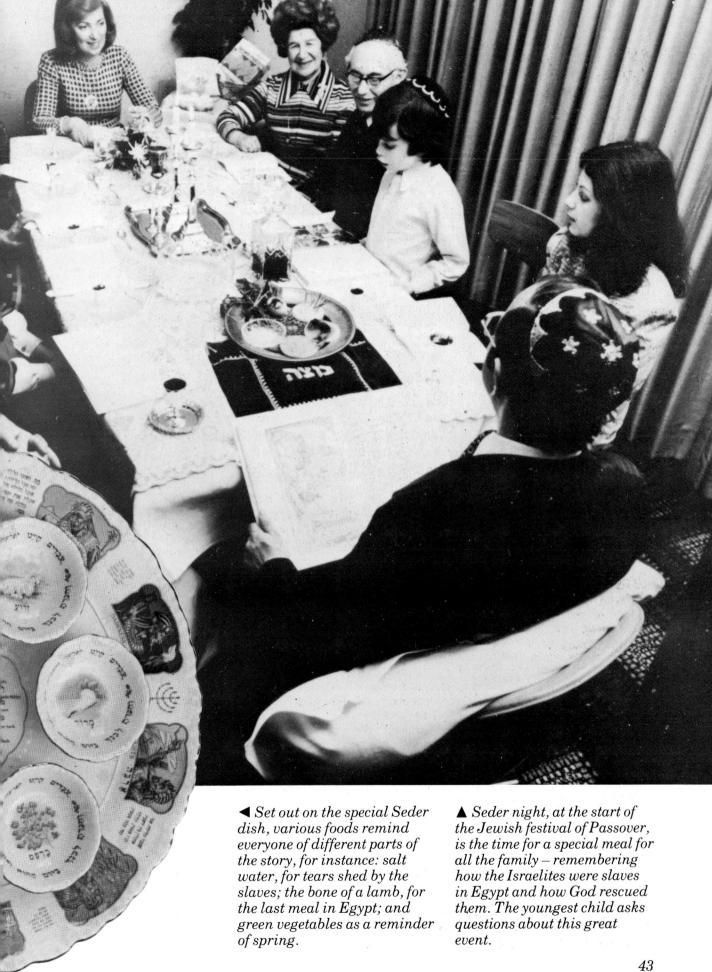

◀ *Set out on the special Seder dish, various foods remind everyone of different parts of the story, for instance: salt water, for tears shed by the slaves; the bone of a lamb, for the last meal in Egypt; and green vegetables as a reminder of spring.*

▲ *Seder night, at the start of the Jewish festival of Passover, is the time for a special meal for all the family – remembering how the Israelites were slaves in Egypt and how God rescued them. The youngest child asks questions about this great event.*

43

Purim: Jewish

LONG AGO THERE LIVED a great and mighty king who ruled a vast empire from Persia to India and Ethiopia. The king Ahazareus, longed for a faithful wife, so he ordered all the most beautiful women to come to the palace. One of these was a women called Esther and, when the king saw her, he fell in love with her and made her his Queen. Esther was a Jew, but she kept this secret from the king.

Now also at the palace was a proud and wicked nobleman called Haman. One day he grew angry because a Jew called Mordecai refused to bow down before him. So great and terrible was his fury, that he decided to kill Mordecai and all the Jews. By telling lies about the Jews, he gained the king's permission to send orders to all of the empire that, on a certain day, every Jew was to be killed. Haman had chosen the day by casting lots, called 'pur'.

When Mordecai heard this he wept, and, as he was a relative of Queen Esther, she soon heard about the wicked plot. Dressed in her finest robes, she went to see the king. So beautiful was she, he offered to grant any request she might make. Esther invited the king and Haman to dine with her and, while they were eating, Esther told the king that an evil man was plotting to murder all her people. The king demanded, 'Who is this man?' 'Haman', replied Esther. Then the king knew that Haman had lied about the Jews and he ordered that Haman should be executed. So, through Esther, the Jews were saved and great was the rejoicing that day.

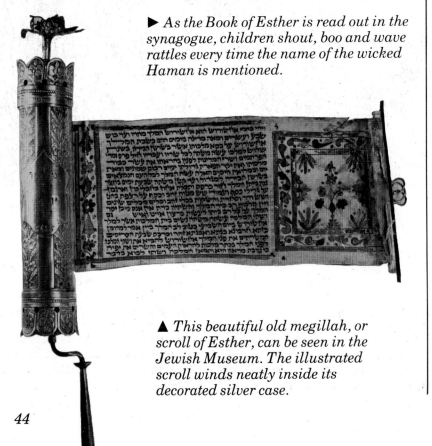

▶ *As the Book of Esther is read out in the synagogue, children shout, boo and wave rattles every time the name of the wicked Haman is mentioned.*

▲ *This beautiful old megillah, or scroll of Esther, can be seen in the Jewish Museum. The illustrated scroll winds neatly inside its decorated silver case.*

When? Purim, so called after the 'pur', the lots which Haman cast, falls on the 14th of Adar each year (February–March). This was the day chosen by Haman for the murder of the Jews.

What happens? The festival centres on the reading of the story of Queen Esther, Mordecai and Haman which is to be found in the Book of Esther. This book is read on the evening before (the start of

the festival day) and in the morning, either in the synagogue or at home. But what a reading! It can sound like a riot because, every time the name of Haman is read out, everyone boos and shouts trying to drown out his evil name.

In some places a great carnival takes place through the streets with a huge model of Haman which is booed and hissed, before finally being burned to loud cheers.

Children dress up in fancy dress and gifts are given at the parties. It is a noisy, cheerful time as everyone remembers the downfall of Haman.

A SPECIAL BISCUIT is baked at Purim. It is a three-cornered shape and filled with poppy seeds. It is called a 'haman-tashen' and is supposed to look like Haman's

hat or, some people say, like his ears!

Why? The festival of Purim celebrates the deliverance of the Jews from a terrible plot. Throughout history the Jews have been attacked by evil people (like Hitler). Yet the Jewish people have survived and at Purim, this survival is joyfully celebrated.

45

When? The birthday of Rama, Rama Naumi, occurs on the ninth day of the 'bright fortnight' of the month Chaitra in March or April.

What happens? For eight days before the ninth of the bright fortnight, people will fast for various periods of time and, at the same time, there will be a constant recital of the great story about Rama, the Ramayana. The Ramayana has 25,000 verses.

On the ninth day, the main stories of Rama are read and sometimes acted as well. Offerings of food, but not of flour or other grains, are made.

NO FLOUR or any grain is eaten on this day, but the fast is broken with fruits – oranges, bananas and so forth, and with a wide variety of nuts.

Why? The Ramayana, meaning the Way of Rama, is the great moral, ethical and religious foundation of Hindu life. All couples would like to model themselves on Rama and his wife Sita. In the Ramayana, the great theme of good triumphing over

Rama Naumi: Hindu

IN A TIME BEYOND time there lived on earth two creatures of great importance. One was the devil king Ravana, lord of all he desired, and enemy of gods and men alike. The other was king Dasaratha who ruled the beautiful kingdom of Ayodhya. Dasaratha was 60,000 years old, but yet he had no sons. So he ordered sacrifices to the gods to grant him sons.

In Heaven, the gods were in chaos. Demon king Ravana had attacked Heaven and it seemed nothing could stop him for one special reason. Brahma, supreme God, had granted Ravana one wish: that no god nor anything from the underworld would ever be able to kill him. So Ravana had attacked Heaven and the gods were in confusion.

Then a scheme came to them. Ravana had so little regard for men, that he had not included them in Brahma's promise. What if one of the gods were to become a man, or even men – surely, then, those men could kill Ravana?

At just this moment, the smoke from old king Dasaratha's sacrifice fires reached Heaven. What better than that the mighty god Vishnu should answer Dasaratha's prayer and be born as his sons?

So Vishnu descended and was born to Dasaratha's two wives. They had four sons, of which Rama and Lakshmana were the most important, for they, and most particularly Rama, were to end the life of evil Ravana and free all creation from his terror.

▲ *Rama travels to his wedding. For Hindus, Rama and his wife, Sita, are the model couple.*

▶ *A dancer in Bengal dressed as the ten-headed Ravana.*

evil is stressed again – and so it is natural to rejoice at Rama's most special birth.

Rosh Hashanah and

Yom Kippur: Jewish

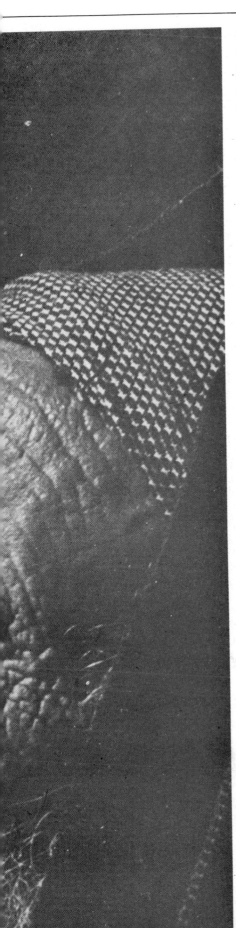

ON THE FIRST DAY of the month Tishri, the Lord God decided to start making the world. You could call the first of Tishri the birthday of the world. God created the heavens and the earth and there was darkness still over all. So God ordered light to appear and he divided the dark times from the light times and called them day and night. Then God divided the waters and created dry land. On this dry land he created plants and trees, while in the heavens he made stars, the sun and the moon, so we could tell when the great festivals should come. Then he brought forth all the animals and birds which swarmed over the dry land. And God looked and saw that it was good. Last of all he created man and woman in his own image and gave them the world to care for and again he saw that it was good. On the seventh day he rested. But seven days of God's time is not like seven of our days, rather it is like a vast spread of time.

Also on the first of Tishri it is said that Abraham bound his son Isaac to prepare to sacrifice him as God had commanded. But God was only testing Abraham's love and Isaac was freed.

When? Rosh Hashanah (New Year) starts on the first day of the month Tishri. Yom Kippur falls nine days later. These festivals fall between September and October. This period is called Yamim Noraim – the Days of Awe.

What happens? Rosh Hashanah, the New Year, is a rather solemn day – for the purpose of it is to remember all the failures and faults of the last year. The festival focuses on the service in the synagogue when the shofar, a ram's horn, is blown. The mournful sound calls everyone to pray for forgiveness. The traditional greeting is 'May you be written and sealed for a good year' and many New Year cards are sent.

◄ *The blowing of the shofar, the ram's horn, is the great moment of the Jewish New Year service – Rosh Hashanah. The solemn sound calls everyone present to pray for forgiveness and a new start.*

Nine days later, Yom Kippur brings this time of repentance to a close. It is a fast day and is the most important day in the Jewish year. Before coming to the synagogue, you must seek forgiveness from anyone you have harmed. After a ritual bath, everyone goes to the synagogue to sing the Kol Nidrei, the ending of old vows in order to prepare for the demands of a new year. This takes place in the evening. All the next day there are services with readings from the Torah, and also from the Book of Jonah – a symbol of forgiveness by God. The festival ends with the final blowing of the shofar.

AS YOM KIPPUR is a fast day, it is Rosh Hashanah which provides interesting food. Bread and apples are dipped in honey – for a sweet year, and some groups eat a head of a sheep or fish, to ensure the year puts them ahead!

Why? The covenant with God, of being his people, means that failings offend God and the people need to show their sorrow and accept God's forgiveness.

49

Wesak: Buddhist

When? Wesak (Visakha) is on the full moon day of the month Visakha – usually in May or June.

What happens? A large puja or act of worship is held, which is why the festival is sometimes called Visakha Puja. Extra hospitality and generosity is shown to the monks in order that the donors may gain more merit to help with a better rebirth. Often captured birds, fish or turtles are released to show the love and compassion of the Buddha. Homes and temples are hung with lanterns and flowers, and flower offerings are placed before the statues of Buddha. In the evening, processions go round the temple with incense sticks, lit candles and flowers, before the day ends with a night-long sermon which tells of the great teachings of Buddha.

THE FESTIVAL is not a feast day, so there are no special foods.

Why? The teachings of the Buddha and the order of monks which he founded are the heart of Buddhism. The linking of the three main events of Buddha's life on one day gives an occasion for remembering his teaching.

◄ *All the great events in Prince Siddhatha's life occurred on the same day in different years. He was born, enlightened and died on Wesak day. In this sculpture Buddha is lying on his side as he prepares to die.*

► *At Buddhist festivals, it is the custom to give alms (gifts) to the monks. In this way, the giver earns merit and is helped to a better rebirth. Here is a monk in Britain with some of his Wesak gifts.*

IN THE OLDEN DAYS of India, there was born, on the full moon day of the month of Visakha, a wondrous child called Prince Siddhatha. At his birth he walked and talked and amazed all. Siddhatha's father knew his son would be great – but a wise man told him that Siddhatha would not be a king, but a monk. His father, the king, did not want a monk for a son. So he kept Siddhatha within a beautiful palace where everything that he wanted was provided.

Siddhatha grew up happily and married. But one day, wishing to see what lay beyond the palace wall, he persuaded his charioteer to take him out into the city. As they rode, Siddhatha saw four sights which he had never seen before: an old man, a sick man, a dead body and a wandering monk. Each time he saw one of these sights he asked his charioteer what it meant. Siddhatha was very disturbed to learn that he would grow old, be sick and die.

From that day on, he decided to become a monk. Leaving his family at dead of night he went into the forest, to try and find out what life meant.

After many years, he was no nearer finding the answer. Then, on the day of the full moon of the month of Visakha, as he sat beneath the Bodhi tree, he understood all and became the Enlightened One, the Buddha.

For the next forty-five years he taught his followers how to understand life and how to break free from the sufferings of life. At long last, he came to die. He died on the day of the full moon of the month of Visakha.

Whitsun: Christian

When? Whitsun (Pentecost) comes seven weeks after Easter Sunday. It therefore falls between May and June in the Western church, and in June to July in the Eastern church.

What happens? Pentecost – seven weeks – is one name for this festival. The other name, 'Whit Sunday', arises from the custom of admitting new members to the church on this day. They all wore white – hence 'white' or 'whit' Sunday. In some areas it is still common to have a procession from the church, which goes out around the parish bounds – taking the message out, just as the twelve burst out of their room and went into the streets. Great Whitsun banners are made, often with the symbols of the Holy Spirit on them; flames and the dove being most popular.

THERE IS NO DISH that everyone eats at Whitsun but there are some local ones such as the traditional Gloucestershire 'white pot' – a pudding made of treacle, milk, flour and brown sugar.

Why? Christians believe Jesus to be the Son of God. When Jesus rose from the dead, he returned to God. But he sent the third aspect of God, the Holy Spirit, to move people, to fire them with love of God. Through the Holy Spirit, Christians believe Jesus is at work within them.

◀ *The Christian festival of Whitsun recalls the day that the Holy Spirit (shown here as a dove) was sent to the disciples of Jesus. They saw 'tongues of fire' falling.*

▶ *A grand Whit Walk processes through the centre of Manchester led by the Rose Queens, who come from churches in the area.*

IN A SMALL ROOM, hidden away from sight, the twelve friends of Jesus sat in fear. So many strange things had happened. Their beloved friend and teacher had been killed, buried – and had risen again, had walked and talked with them. But then he had risen into Heaven promising to send power to them. What power they did not know and, just at this moment, they were frightened and uncertain.

The next moment the room shook. A great force, like rushing wind, filled the room and tongues of fire descended onto the heads of the friends – but did not burn them. Instantly, the twelve friends were filled with joy and to their amazement found that they could all speak and understand all the languages of the world.

Rushing out into the street they began to speak about Jesus, and about God's love, and whether those listening spoke Greek, or Latin, Hebrew or any other language, they could understand what the friends were saying. Then Peter, one of the closest of Jesus' friends, told the people the whole story of Jesus. On that day, the day when the Holy Spirit descended, no less than three thousand people joined them to become followers of Jesus.

Rites of Passage

RITES OF PASSAGE is a phrase invented by anthropologists to describe all those ceremonies which mark the various stages of life. Just as festivals mark the cycle of the year, so rites of passage mark the life cycle of individuals.

There are four major rites of passage: birth, initiation, marriage, death. Around these great turning points in people's lives, religious rituals have been woven. These have two functions. Firstly, they help the person and his or her family to accept the changes. Secondly, they are used to help teach or remind people of the great fundamental beliefs of the faith. Take death, for instance. It is necessary for the family and friends to mourn, to dispose of the body and then to try to return to normal life. Religious ceremonies help with this. But death is also the point at which beliefs in the after-life, in reincarnation or resurrection can be most forcefully taught.

Not all religions treat the rites of passage in this way. Buddhism in particular does not really observe birth, marriage or death. Therefore I have not included it among the other rites, but have written a summary of how and why it is so different (see page 80).

Likewise, not all faiths have initiation rites. Initiation rites are ceremonies which mark the change from child to adult. I have grouped together the three chief initiation rites (Christian, Jewish and Sikh) and you will find an account of these on page 61.

There is only space to describe here the major rituals which occur in Britain, or are related to groups which now live in Britain. When dealing with Christianity I have only written about Roman Catholic and Anglican practice, with occasional reference to wider protestant ceremonies. It would have been impossible to try and cover Orthodox rituals as well.

▼ *Passage through life from childhood to old age is marked by ceremonies called 'rites of passage'.*

▲ *This little boy is holding a model of an old coin with 'Happy New Year' written on it. Like all Chinese people, he is a year older each New Year's Day – no matter when he was born.*

Chinese

BIRTH RITES

CHINESE STORIES say that the whole of the world was born from a great cosmic egg which split open to produce the earth and the sky. As a symbol of the start of all births, special red eggs are given at the Full Month feast which is described below.

The stories also say that the evil spirits are jealous and angry when a baby is born because of the happiness which babies – especially baby boys – bring. So the spirits are thought to steal the babies. Perhaps in the past this was one way of explaining why so many babies died. To trick the evil spirits, it has become a tradition not to name the baby for thirty days. After thirty days a great feast is held at which the baby is given a name. But it is not an ordinary name – but a silly or odd name. So the baby might be called 'Pig Face' or, if it is a boy, given a girl's name. The idea is that the evil spirit, hearing such

美
花

Beautiful Flower

狗
面

Dog Face

▲ *To trick the evil spirits, Chinese parents give their babies odd names like these.*

names, will not be interested in stealing such a worthless baby. As Chinese children are given different names at different times of their life, it is not a problem to give such odd names.

What happens . . .
At birth, the exact time of the birth is carefully recorded. This will be used to cast the horoscope, the fortune, of the child. Chinese do not celebrate birthday anniversaries. All Chinese are one year older on New Year's Day. The Chinese also say you are one year old the day you are born. So a baby born on the day before New Year would be officially two years old the next morning.

After thirty days, the great feast of Full Month, or One Month, is held. The baby is properly welcomed by family and friends and given the trick name to confuse the evil spirits who might want to steal it. Many wonderful dishes of food are served, but most special of all are the red eggs, symbols of good luck (red) and creation and birth (the egg).

While babies are always welcome – it is true to say that boys are especially welcome, because they will carry on the family name.

Birth

Christian

BIRTH RITES

WATER is a very powerful symbol in Christianity. It reminds Christians of the chaos of the Flood of Noah; of how Moses divided the water to bring the Israelites out of slavery in Egypt; of the new life which comes when the rain falls; of how Jesus himself was baptised in the river Jordan at the start of his preaching. Christians use water as a symbol of new life. In the baptism of babies (or, if they are Baptists who disagree with infant baptism, adults), Christians see the water as washing away the old sinful nature of the person so that the new, Christ-filled person can come out. Christians believe that somehow we have fallen away from doing God's will. This is often explained by telling the story of how Adam and Eve disobeyed God in the Garden of Eden. This myth tries to explain how evil and suffering came into the world. Through Jesus, Christians believe they can come back to God and baptism is the way this is formally done.

▼ *At the naming of Christian babies, water is used to symbolise the washing away of sin and evil. In the name of God the Father, Son and Holy Spirit, the priest pours water from the font onto the baby's head three times. And so the child is named and welcomed into the Church.*

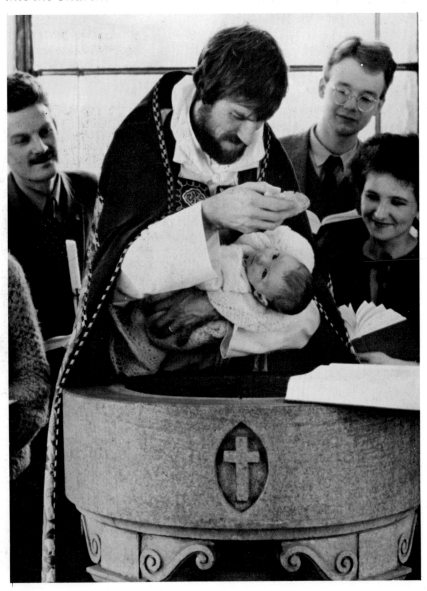

What happens . . .
The ceremony takes place in church and is an occasion to celebrate the birth and welcome the child into the church. The baby is usually dressed in white – symbol of being clean and pure. As well as the parents, there will be godparents who take the vows on behalf of the baby who obviously cannot take them him or herself. The godparents have a special responsibility to help to bring the baby up to be a Christian.

The parents and godparents declare their belief in the Christian faith and promise to teach the child about Christianity. Then the water in the font, a special container (usually carved from stone), is blessed. Holding the baby, the priest asks the parents to name the child. Then, scooping the water out with a shell, he pours it onto the baby's head three times, baptising the child in the name of the Holy Trinity: Father, Son and Holy Spirit. A lighted candle is given to show that light outshines darkness and evil. The sign of the cross is made on the baby's forehead to show he or she is now a follower of Jesus. The child is then welcomed into the church community.

The service is followed by a christening party with a large fruit cake (sometimes this is the top layer of the wedding cake which has been specially saved). The word 'christening' comes from 'Christ-naming'.

Birth

Hindu

BIRTH RITES

HINDUS BELIEVE that our souls have lived many lives before this life, and, unless you are extremely holy in this life, you will have to live through hundreds or thousands of reincarnations – more lives, not always as a human being. The sort of life you are born into, animal or human, good or bad, is the result of Karma – what you did in your earlier lives. A good earlier life brings a good rebirth. To help the soul through yet another life, and eventually to stop rebirth altogether, Hindus mark the course of life by sixteen special stages – called samskara. The idea is that the ritual at each stage will help to improve your Karma.

As birth is the very start of another rebirth, it is obviously a very special time.

What happens . . .

To help make as good a rebirth as possible, some Hindu parents will ask a priest to find the best day to have sexual intercourse and thus to start the rebirth. This is the first samskara. When the mother is pregnant, she will recite verses from the Hindu scriptures, so the child in her womb is surrounded by good words. This is the second samskara. She will also eat special foods which are not too salty or spicy – which might harm the baby. This is the third samskara.

When the baby is born, careful note is taken of the time and day, as this will be needed to cast the baby's horoscope – fortune. The fourth samskara is the washing of the baby. Then a golden pen or rod is dipped in honey and the syllable 'aum' the ultimate sound of the Universe, the essence of God is written on the baby's tongue. Hindus say the syllable 'aum' before prayer, so this prepares the child for a life of truth and worship.

Once the horoscope has been cast by a priest, he will tell the parents which syllables would be most suitable for a name. At the naming ceremony (the fifth samskara) a special food called 'prasadam' is made from nuts, sweets and fruit and shared out. The sixth, seventh and eighth samskaras are the baby's first outing into the sunlight; the first time the baby eats solid food and finally, for some, the piercing of the ear lobes.

The ninth and final ceremony for birth is when the hair of the child – between a few months and a couple of years old – is completely cut off to symbolise the desire to remove bad Karma carried over from previous lives, and the hope that the child will lead a good life.

▲ *This pregnant Hindu mother is reading to her unborn baby.*

▼ *Hindu boy babies have their hair shaved off to remove any bad luck carried over from their previous life.*

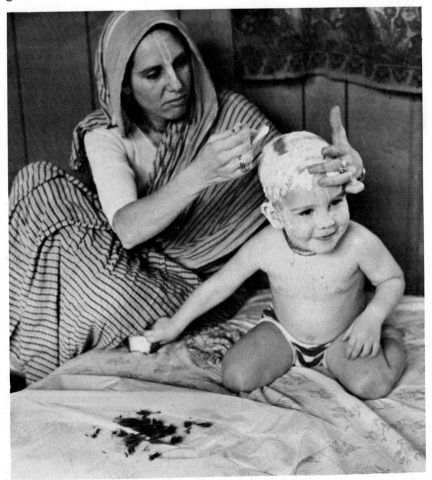

Birth

Jewish

BIRTH RITES

THE MOST HOLY SCRIPTURES of Judaism, the Torah, tell how Abraham, long, long ago, left his own city to follow the One God. It tells how God made a special agreement with Abraham – a Covenant. God promised that Abraham would be the father of nations and that his people would live in Canaan forever. As a sign of this Covenant, and their love of God, God ordered that all boy babies must be circumcised – have the foreskin of their penis cut off. This has been observed since then by the Jews. Thus every Jewish man carries on his body a physical reminder of the Covenant.

Legend also has it that the great prophet of old, Elijah, likes to attend every circumcision ceremony – so a chair is set out for him called 'The Throne of Elijah'.

What happens . . .

The ritual of circumcision is called Brit Milah – the Covenant of Circumcision. It must take place eight days after the baby is born, even if the day is the Sabbath or Holy Day. The ceremony takes place at home and the circumcision is done by a qualified person called a mohel. When the baby is carried into the room, he is greeted with 'Blessed is he'. The mohel takes the baby, places him briefly on the Throne of Elijah and then hands the baby to the sandek – the godfather. He holds him during the ceremony. The mohel says a blessing which recalls the Covenant and then cuts the foreskin off the penis while the sandek holds the baby. The father gives a blessing, thanking God for his Commandment and announcing the entry of the boy into the Covenant of Abraham. The rest wish him a good life, worthy marriage, and hope the

▲ *At the Jewish circumcision ceremony, the mohel (the person who carries out the operation) gives the baby a drop of wine as a blessing.*

boy will make a good student of the Torah – Holy Books.

Finally the Kiddush blessing is said – the thanksgiving for God who creates the vine – and then wine is handed round – even the baby gets some. At this point the baby is named for the first time with these words: 'His name shall be called in Israel . . . the son of . . .'. The service is followed by a celebration meal, the Seudat Mitzvah, 'feast of the fulfilment of a commandment'.

For girls there is, of course, no circumcision. On the first Sabbath after the baby's birth, the girl's father announces the child's name publicly in the synagogue and invites everyone to a kiddush – a light meal of celebration.

Muslim

BIRTH RITES

MUHAMMAD, the prophet of Allah, taught many things about children. He showed that circumcision – cutting the foreskin off the penis -- was the sign and practice of all the prophets of Allah, starting with Abraham who circumcised his son Isaac. Muhammad also taught that shaving the head and sacrificing one or two sheep, the ritual of Aqeeqah, would protect the child from disasters.

The summons to prayer, one of the five pillars of Islamic belief, is the Adhan, called from the tops of mosques to let the faithful know that prayer is about to start. The Adhan contains the fundamental beliefs of Islam: 'I bear witness that there is no God but Allah and Muhammad is the Prophet of Allah' and this is whispered into the baby's ear at birth so that the first words the child hears are these basic beliefs.

What happens . . .

After the baby is born and has been washed, the father or the Imam will immediately whisper the Adhan into the baby's right ear. Into the left ear is whispered the Iqamat (the minor Adhan), which is almost identical but contains the extra line – 'Come to prayer'. These words will ring in the child's ears throughout his or her lifetime.

When the baby comes home, the second ceremony takes place. This is called Tahneek. A small piece of sugar, date or honey is put in the mouth of the baby – usually by the oldest or most respected member of the family. It is hoped that this sweetness will make the child both kind and obedient. The ceremony finishes with a personal prayer to Allah.

Seven days after birth, two final ceremonies are held. The first is called the Aqeeqah and this is when the baby is named. Part of the Aqeeqah ritual is the shaving of the baby's head – a symbol of the removal of uncleanliness. The hair is then weighed and silver of the same weight is given as charity (zakat) to the poor. The Aqeeqah ceremony finishes with the holding of a feast, at which one or two goats or sheep (two for a boy – one for a girl) are sacrificed and cooked and shared with the visitors and the poor.

The second ceremony of this seventh day is for boy babies and is Khitan – circumcision. Performed either by the father or an Imam, this recalls Abraham and his son Isaac. If the baby is not well, then circumcision can be delayed, but it must be done in the first few months.

▼ *All Muslim children have the Adhan (the call to prayer) whispered into their ears very soon after birth.*

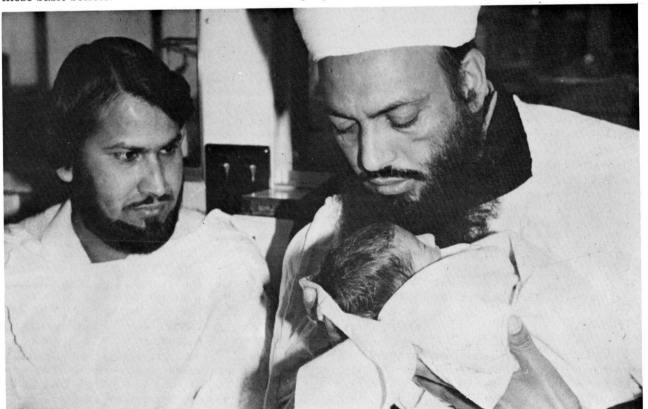

Birth

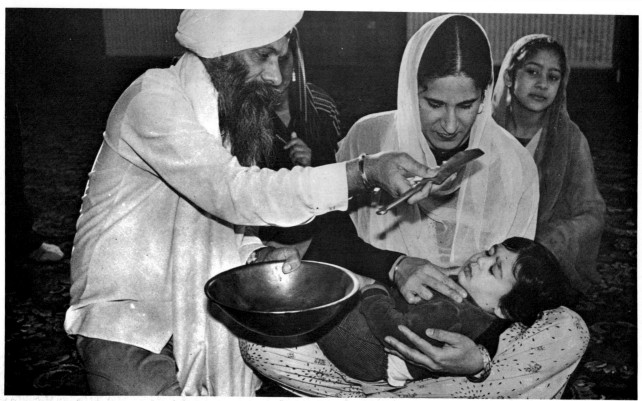

▲ *At a Sikh naming ceremony, the baby's tongue is touched with a sword which has been dipped in the special sacred drink – amrit.*

Sikh

BIRTH RITES

FOR SIKHS, God and the equality of all people, men, women, rich, poor are of great importance. In the birth ceremonies this is shown in a number of ways. The first words the baby will hear are those of the Mool Mantra: 'There is One God, Eternal Truth is his name; maker of all and present in all. Fearing and hating nothing, timeless is his image; not born and not dying; by the grace of the Guru, made known'. This sums up Sikh beliefs. Likewise, when the naming ceremony takes place at the temple (gurdwara) the sharing of the special food (karah parshad) and the use of the only two surnames (Singh for boys, Kaur for girls) instead of the caste surnames of Hinduism, show the belief in equality, which was so powerfully taught by Guru Gobind Singh (see Baisakhi, on page 8).

What happens . . .
At birth, the baby is washed and the words of the Mool Mantra, the first verses of the Holy Scriptures, the Guru Granth Sahib, are whispered into the baby's ear. Then a drop of honey is placed on the tip of the baby's tongue as a symbol of kind and pure words. Some weeks later, the baby will be brought to the gurdwara to be named. The ceremony takes place before the congregation as they are the ones who officially accept and welcome the child. The parents bring three gifts: butter, sugar and flour to make the karah parshad which is shared out at all services; some ingredients for the free meal which follows the service; and finally a richly embroidered cloth called a romala to cover the Holy Book, the Guru Granth Sahib.

The family gather round the Guru Granth Sahib. Amrit is made by mixing sugar crystals with water. A double-edged sword, one of the symbols of Sikhism, is dipped into the amrit and, after prayers and the reading of the Mool Mantra, the baby's tongue is touched by the dripping sword. The mother drinks the rest of the amrit.

Now the Guru Granth Sahib is opened at random and the hymn on the left hand page is sung. The first letter of this hymn will be the first letter of the baby's name. The parents quickly discuss what name it will be and the Granthi (priest) or family announce the choice to the congregation, adding either Singh (for a boy) or Kaur (for a girl) as the surname. The congregation then welcomes the named child and, after further hymns and prayers, everyone shares in the karah parshad – symbol of equality – and ends up in the langar (free kitchen) to share the celebratory meal.

Not all the faiths we have looked at have initiation rites, but three do: Judaism has the bar mitzvah; Christianity has confirmation; and Sikhism has entry into the Khalsa.

Christian

INITIATION RITES

IT IS RATHER DIFFICULT to define confirmation as a straight initiation rite. To begin with, it does not always happen when someone is crossing from childhood into adulthood. People who are converted to Christianity in later life will still go through confirmation if they become a Roman Catholic or Anglican. So they could be aged anywhere between eighteen and eighty! Furthermore, Roman Catholics have a series of rituals which start with first confession at about the age of seven, go through first communion aged between seven and eight and culminate in confirmation in the early teens. In the Anglican church, it is usual for people to be confirmed in their early teens, marking more the transition from childhood to adulthood. In the Anglican church, confirmation leads to first communion.

The word 'confirmation' explains the basis of the ritual. It is the occasion when the individual confirms the vows and promises to God which were made on his or her behalf at baptism. The individual is now old enough and mature enough to take these commitments and beliefs on him or herself. Therefore, in the Baptist church, which does not believe in infant baptism, it is not confirmation which takes place in early teens, but baptism, as the individual is now capable of understanding the vows and commitments.

What happens . . .

Before confirmation takes place, the candidates attend confirmation classes where they are taught the Christian beliefs. It is important to note that they are only candidates. It is up to the priest, and/or bishop, to decide whether they are mature enough to be confirmed.

The service of confirmation takes place before the whole congregation and has to be conducted by a bishop. It is the bishop who asks the candidates to affirm their belief in the Christian faith and who then places his hands on their heads as, one by one, they kneel before him. In the name of the Trinity he gives the power of the Holy Spirit, the third aspect of the Trinity, and through him the candidate becomes part of an unbroken chain reaching right back to the first Apostles, the disciples of Jesus.

After the ceremony, there is normally a party to which all the candidates and their families as well as the congregation and bishop go. Gifts are also given, marking the shift from childhood to adulthood as in the bar mitzvah. However, confirmation does not give the candidate total equality of status with the other adults as the bar mitzvah does. This comes gradually.

▼ *The bishop asks the confirmation candidates to affirm their belief in the Christian faith and then places his hands on their heads as they kneel before him.*

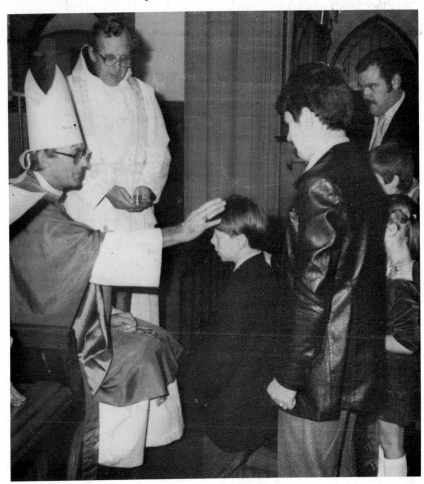

Initiation

Jewish

INITIATION RITES

AMONGST THE ORTHODOX JEWS it is only boys who have an initiation ceremony known as bar mitzvah. The name means son (bar) of the Commandment (mitzvah). Reform and Liberal Jews also have an initiation ceremony for girls called bat mitzvah, daughter of the Commandment.

Under Jewish law, once a boy reaches thirteen and girl reaches twelve, they are considered adults and can play a full adult part in the life of the community and synagogue. The ceremony of bat and bar mitzvah is the ritualised way of acknowledging this changed status. The ceremony comes at the end of a long period of study and training, particularly in the religious language of Judaism, Hebrew. The Torah (Five Books of Moses) in the synagogue, are always written in Hebrew.

What happens . . .
On the particular Sabbath chosen for the boy's mitzvah, he is called up from the congregation to read the portion of the Torah set for that day. Before reading he says a special bar mitzvah prayer when he promises to keep God's commandments and to be responsible for all his actions before God. Then, perhaps wearing for the first time his prayer shawl, called a tallit, he reads the Torah out loud. Many boys find it a very nerve-racking experience. When the text has been read, the boy returns to his seat while the rabbi preaches about the new responsibilities which the boy, now a man, has taken upon himself. Finally, a lovely blessing is said, which you can find in the Bible (Numbers 6. 24-26) and which was first used by Aaron in the Wilderness when the tribes of Israel had just left slavery in Egypt.

Immediately after the service, there will be kiddush held in the synagogue. This is a blessing of the fruit of the vine (wine) and the serving of a light buffet. It is usually followed by a very splendid feast with many guests, at which the young man is given a whole range of presents which often symbolise his move into adulthood (perhaps a bank account, briefcase and prayer books). Unlike some rites of initiation, this rite takes place automatically at the age of thirteen for boys and twelve for girls. From that day on, they are treated as full adults. For instance, it is necessary to have ten Jewish men present, called a minyan, before any service can start. Once a boy has been bar mitzvahed, he is counted as being able to make up the ten necessary for minyan.

◀ *At his bar mitzvah, a Jewish boy has to read from the Torah – in Hebrew. Here he is practising for the great day.*

▶ *At bar mitzvah, Jewish boys wear the 'tefillin' for the first time. These are small black boxes containing words from the Torah. One is bound to the arm and one to the forehead.*

Initiation

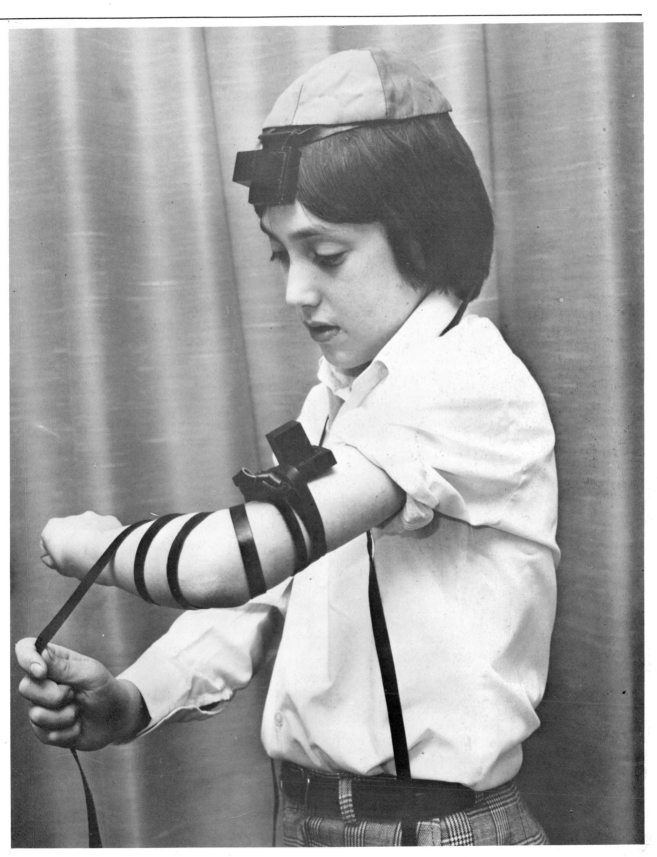

Initiation

Sikh

INITIATION RITES

SIKHISM IS VERY SIMILAR to Christianity in terms of the significance of the entry into the Khalsa, in that you can join the Khalsa at any stage in your life, once you have passed through childhood. It is not uncommon for young people aged between fourteen and sixteen to seek admission to the Khalsa. But it is not an automatic right. Once someone has sought entry and the members of the Khalsa feel that the person is trying to live the Sikh way of life, then the ceremony can proceed. The ceremony is a private event. It often takes place in the gurdwara (temple) but can be held anywhere as long as there is a copy of the Holy Scriptures, the Guru Granth Sahib, present. The ceremony is called amrit sanskar or pahul and can occur at any time of the year, though it is usually done at the time of the festival of Baisakhi (see page 8). It is conducted by five members of the Khalsa who must be properly attired with the five Ks. These are five objects which the founder of the Khalsa, Guru Gobind Singh gave to his followers (see page 8).

What happens . . .

The ceremony begins with the opening of the Guru Granth Sahib and with an outline of the fundamentals of the Sikh faith by one of the five. (The candidates and the five can be men or women.) Then amrit is made from a mixture of sugar crystals and water. The candidates then say 'The Khalsa is of God and the Victory is to God' and drink a handful of amrit. It is then sprinkled on their eyes and hair and this is repeated five times. The Mool Mantra (see page 60), summing up the basic Sikh beliefs, is then chanted. The ceremony ends with the prayer Ardas and with the traditional sharing out of the religious food, karah parshad, symbolising the equality and universality of the Sikh faith. If a Sikh fails in his or her way of life and falls short of the Sikh standards, then he or she has to undergo the intitiation ceremony again.

It can be seen from the variety of attitudes and rituals that initiation ceremonies have very different rôles in the different faiths. While they do often emphasise the shift from child to adult, this is not always the case.

▶ *Entry into the Khalsa, the special community of Sikhism, is a private ceremony. The person joining the Khalsa is sprinkled with the sacred drink, amrit.*

Chinese

MARRIAGE RITES

CHINESE BELIEF teaches that the world is moved and kept active by two forces. These two forces are exact opposites and are always struggling with each other. But they also need each other. They are called yin and yang. Yin is usually described as female: dark, watery and quiet. Yang as male: light, fiery and active. These two forces are in everything – so it is quite natural that they should play a very major rôle as symbols in marriage. The two forces are represented by the dragon (yang – male) and the phoenix (yin – female).

When she marries, a woman leaves her family and is no longer seen as being part of her own family. Instead she becomes a part of her husband's family and she is expected to produce sons so that the family can continue.

What happens . . .

In the past, all marriages were arranged by a go-between. Nowadays, the couple will often have met independently, but it is still customary to gain the approval of the families. Traditionally there are six rituals which have to be observed to ensure a good marriage. Firstly, the bridegroom's family offers a gift to the bride's family, such as food, wine and money. If this is accepted, usually by means of a return gift, then the serious negotiations can start.

The second ritual is to exchange horoscopes. If the horoscopes are compatible, then they are placed before the ancestor tablets and various family gods for approval. This is the third ritual.

The fourth ritual is the payment of the bride price. The bride's family has to be compensated for the trouble of bringing up the bride, who is now to leave the family. At this ceremony it is common to have special dragon and phoenix cakes. Once the bride price has been accepted, the betrothal is sealed.

The date of the wedding is chosen by careful attention to the stars – this is the fifth ritual. The wedding itself takes place in the home of the bridegroom. The bride enters, usually wearing a red silk jacket with the yin yang symbols on it. (These also appear on the invitations and decorations for the wedding and on dragon and phoenix cakes.) The marriage consists of prayers and offerings to the bridegroom's ancestors and the household gods. Various other customs, such as the bride weeping as she comes in are also common. This is the sixth ritual and now the bride is part of her new family. It is customary for her to go home three days later to say good-bye and then she returns to her husband.

▲ *The phoenix is the yin symbol. This one comes from a Chinese wedding card.*

▲ *The dragon is the yang symbol. It, too, appears on Chinese wedding cards and invitations.*

Marriage

Christian

MARRIAGE RITES

ALTHOUGH there is little about marriage in the New Testament stories of Jesus, there is the story of the miracle at the wedding feast in the town of Cana. Jesus was there as a guest and, when the wine ran out, he caused jars of water to be turned into wine so that the feast could continue.

In Roman Catholic thinking, marriage is seen as a sacrament. It is part of the often steep and rugged pathway to eternal life. Marriage is viewed as divinely given and as blessed by Jesus' miracle at Cana. While celebacy – not marrying – is seen as perhaps a slightly better way to live, it is recognised that the way most people will live will involve mar-

riage. So marriage is seen as part of the pathway to eternal life.

In Protestant churches, something of this approach still exists, but as there is no celebacy for its clergy, the state of marriage is seen not so much as a sacrament but as a divinely ordained normal way of life.

What happens . . .
In Christianity, the two individuals chose whom they wish to marry – but it is expected that the couple will seek the blessing of their parents. However, as arranged marriages are not part of Christian life, it is perfectly possible to marry in church without the approval of your parents, if you are of age. (Eighteen in England, sixteen in Scotland.) When engaged, the couple will visit the clergyman to discuss not

only the wedding but also marriage with all its responsibilities.

One rôle of the church is to make couples think hard about whether marriage is right yet for them. Then, in England, the clergyman will have to read out the banns, or announcement of the wedding, on three consecutive Sundays beforehand in case anyone knows of a reason why the couple should not marry.

On the wedding day, the bridegroom and his best man – a sort of special helper – will be in the church when the bride, escorted by her father, arrives. The bride normally wears a veil and is dressed in white (a symbol of purity) and is attended by bridesmaids – young girls. Flowers, a sign of fertility, are also carried. The father officially 'gives' the bride to her husband to be.

The couple make their vows to love, honour and cherish each other, in sickness and in health and the vows of marriage are said by each partner and rings are exchanged. The priest will then declare them man and wife. Some couples then have a special communion service – or nuptial mass – when they receive the bread and wine together, in front of the rest of the congregation.

Outside, confetti and rice – symbols of fertility and good luck – are thrown, before everyone goes to the wedding feast for food, speeches and drink.

◀ *In Christian marriage ceremonies, the rings which are given and blessed symbolise unbroken love, faithfulness and eternity.*

▶ *For Christians, a true marriage is one which takes place in church. The priest asks for God's protection and blessing and the couple promise to be faithful.*

Marriage

▲ *Details of the long Hindu wedding ceremony may vary from region to region. This couple are walking round the sacred fire reciting their vows. Their union is symbolised by the cord and cloth.*

Hindu

MARRIAGE RITES

TO HINDU COUPLES, the model for marriage is the love and faithfulness of Rama and Sita, the great heroes of the saga, the Ramayana. Because of their belief in rebirth and in the importance of horoscopes (fortunes) Hindu families normally arrange the marriages of their children, sometimes without the couple meeting until their wedding day. It is felt that the families, who are being united by the marriage, should know best what will lead to a happy marriage.

Hindu weddings are full of symbolism, vows, readings and ritual acts. In the account below I try to cover some of the main ones. There are many local customs which vary from area to area.

What happens . . .

The decision that the couple should marry is taken by the families. It is often finally agreed at a dinner party with six men from each family present. Although dowries are not officially given nowadays, it is customary for the bride's family to pay for the wedding.

The day for the wedding is chosen by an astrologer who examines the horoscopes of the couple in order to chose the most suitable day. The wedding takes place either in the bride's home, or at the temple. The bride will have spent hours, if not days,

preparing with the help of other women. She will have bathed and then painted her feet and hands with delicate patterns done in orange henna. Her sari will be red with gold thread and she will be bedecked with gold jewellery.

Both bride and bridegroom will worship the elephant, Ganesha, god of fortune, on the day before the wedding – usually in their own homes.

The bridegroom is welcomed by the bride's parents and sits under a colourful decorated canopy called a mandaps. Here the father of the bride will offer him various symbols of happiness, fertility, good life, food and safety. When the bridegroom has been welcomed, the bride is brought in to sit under the mandaps. The family trees of the two people are read out. Then the right hands of the bride and groom are tied together, holy water is sprinkled over them and the father of the bride gives his daughter to the bridegroom.

Next comes the lighting of the sacred arti flame. The couple make offerings of rice, symbol of fertility, to the fire. Then the bride touches a stone, and prayers for her to be as firm as the stone are made, symbolising her break with her own family and her importance as a member of her new family. Then the couple take seven steps around the sacred fire. Only when these steps have been completed are they finally married. The seven steps stand for: food, strength, wealth, fortune, children, happy seasons, friendships and offering of proper sacrifices.

Now they are married and, after prayers and readings, the wedding feast takes place.

▼ *The Hindu priest, using water as a sacred symbol, performs part of the complex Hindu wedding ceremony. On the left the special ceremonial food can be seen.*

Marriage

Jewish

MARRIAGE RITES

'BE FRUITFUL, MULTIPLY AND FILL THE EARTH.' This is the basic teaching behind marriage in Judaism. When God created male and female; when he blessed Noah after the Flood; when he made his Covenant with Abraham, the same words were said: 'Be fruitful'. So marriage and having children is considered one of the most important responsibilities of a Jew. Not to marry is to be seen as disobeying God.

A marriage is not just two people coming together, but two families. So the views of the families are very important. In the past, and amongst some very traditional groups today, the marriages were arranged by a professional marriage maker – a shadkhan.

What happens . . .

On the Sabbath before the wedding, the bridegroom reads the portion of the Torah for that day in the synagogue. He is then cheered to cries of 'mazal tov' – good luck.

The wedding will often take place on a Sunday – it cannot be on a Sabbath (Saturday) or feast day. In the synagogue a special canopy – the chupah – is put up. Supported by four poles it has a fine cloth draped over it and is laden with flowers.

The bride and bridegroom will have fasted from dawn, and now the bridegroom will take his place, facing Jerusalem, under the chupah. Then the bride comes in, led by her mother and mother-in-law to be. Standing together under the chupah the couple listen while the Rabbi pours out a cup of wine and blesses it. The bridegroom then places a gold ring on the bride's forefinger and says: 'Behold you are sanctified to me with this ring, according to the law of Moses and Israel'. The couple are now legally married. A specially prepared document or marriage contract is then read out. It is called a ketubah and is sometimes beautifully illustrated.

Seven marriage blessings are said by the Rabbi. Finally the bridegroom stamps on a wine glass and shatters it to symbolise that even at this happy time they remember the destruction of the Temple of Jerusalem.

At the wedding feast afterwards, it is usual for there to be exciting, lively dancing when the men dance with the bride. The feast ends with grace and a repetition of the seven blessings.

◀ *At the end of the Jewish wedding ceremony, the bridegroom breaks a glass under his foot to recall the sadness all Jews feel at the destruction of their temple in Jerusalem long ago.*

▶ *The Jewish bride and groom are married under the special, decorated canopy (chupah) or, if the congregation are Sefardi Jews, under a prayer shawl held by four men. The canopy symbolises the new home.*

Marriage

Marriage

Muslim

MARRIAGE RITES

THE HOLY QUR'AN expresses the idea of marriage most beautifully. It says: 'And among His signs, is that He has created for you, out of yourselves, wives that you may dwell with them; and has put love and compassion with you'. (30.21)

It is therefore right and proper to marry and to bring up a family who can be taught the ways of Islam.

Most Muslim marriages are arranged. This is because although the two individuals are important, so are the two families, who will now be linked. So the usual procedure is for the man's parents to approach the woman's parents. They will discuss the idea and plan the marriage if it seems right. The final decision rests with the woman, who can refuse.

What happens . . .

When the engagement is finally announced, the two families will formally meet to exchange gifts. It is customary for the bridegroom's family to give the bride's family a dowry. If the bride wishes, she can reduce or cancel the dowry altogether.

Although two Muslims must be witnesses, the marriage is seen as an agreement by the couple, before God – and can therefore take place anywhere. It is usual to hold it in the home.

The wedding ceremony is very short, but the bride takes a long time to prepare for it. A Muslim bride whose family comes from Pakistan or Bangladesh will dress in red trousers and tunic with lots of gold jewellery lent for the occasion. Like Hindu brides, she may paint her hands and feet with orange dye.

If the wedding takes place at

▲ *A Muslim bride may have her hands and feet painted with elaborate, traditional designs.*

home, it is the bride's home. The bridegroom is warmly welcomed by the family and is garlanded with flowers. It is common for the bride to remain in one room, with the bridegroom in another room throughout the service. The Imam and men from both of the families conduct the ceremony which opens with a reading from the fourth surah, or chapter, of the Qur'an. After a short talk on the duties of marriage, the couple then agree to marriage three times, rings are exchanged (the bridegroom's must not be made of gold) and finally the Imam blesses the couple. Together, the couple then lead the guests to the wedding feast.

Marriage

Sikh

MARRIAGE RITES

MARRIAGE is very important for Sikhs. The family is at the centre of Sikh life and it is unusual for people not to marry. But the most important part of the service is not only about marriage itself. It is a great hymn which contains all the major teachings of the Sikh faith. When the daughter of the Fourth Guru (Guru Ram Das) was married, the Guru wrote this hymn, the Lavan. It is sung as the couple circle the Holy Scriptures, the Guru Granth Sahib, four times. At the first circling, the hymn speaks of how, through being a householder, the Sikh can be freed from evil by knowing of God as revealed in the message of the Gurus. At the second circling, the true nature of God is acknowledged and his all-pervading presence throughout the universe is stated. By believing in him, the selfishness of the individual is washed away. At the third circling, the way to be free from the falseness of the world is proclaimed. It is to be achieved through partnership and through the fellowship of Sikh communities. Finally, at the fourth circling, the marriage is used as a kind of picture to describe the union of the soul with God.

What happens . . .

The right choice of a marriage partner is primarily the responsibility of the families. The young people will be consulted, but most of the arrangements will be made by the families.

It is usual to hold the wedding at the gurdwara (temple). It takes place in the morning at the morning worship. The bridegroom, wearing a muslin scarf, sits in front of the Holy Scriptures, the Guru Granth Sahib. The bride, dressed in red trousers and tunic (shalwar and kameez) with a red scarf over her head called a dupatta, and bedecked with gold jewellery, now enters. She will have painted hands and feet and a string of pieces of dried coconut around her neck. These are all symbols of good luck. A chosen person will then read from the Guru Granth Sahib and tell the couple what sort of life they must now lead. Then, after the couple have shown, by bowing to the Guru Granth Sahib, that they agree to marry, the bride's father ties the woman's red scarf – dupatta, to the man's muslin scarf. As the Lavan hymn is sung, the couple walk clockwise around the Guru Granth Sahib four times, stopping and bowing each time. The service ends with the distribution of the sweet food, karah parshad.

After the wedding meal, the couple visit the bride's home and are entertained. Then they move on to the bridegroom's home where the bride is welcomed into the family.

▶ *The Sikh groom's scarf is tied to the bride's scarf. The most important part of a Sikh marriage is the singing of the Lavan – the special wedding hymn.*

Death

Chinese

THE CHINESE have three great religions from which they draw their beliefs about life after death, Confucianism, Taoism and Buddhism. Although they teach very different things about life after death, the Chinese make use of them all, even if to outsiders it seems rather confusing.

The family is so very important to the Chinese, that they cannot imagine life without it. So one belief is that the dead relative goes to live with the other ancestors of the family and from the 'Land of Shades' they watch over the lives of their descendants on earth. To please the ancestors is very important, because otherwise they can cause trouble.

At the same time, there is the belief which comes most strongly from Buddhism. When the soul leaves the body it is judged by the King or Judge of Hell. He decides how good or bad someone has been. Then the soul is sent to serve time in one or more of the Ten Halls of Judgement or Hells. Only after the soul has passed through these Hells can it be reborn on earth in a new body. One way of helping the soul is to provide it with money and goods for the time in Hell – it can then bribe its way out. This is why paper money and models of cars, houses, etc, are burnt at Chinese funerals.

What happens . . .
The body is washed and then dressed in special clothes. The mourners wear white – the colour of mourning. The body is put in a simple wooden coffin and is taken to the graveyard followed by a band of musicians playing drums and cymbols, fireworks are set off to scare evil spirits away. A red strip lies on the coffin, colour of good luck. At the grave the funeral goods, Bank of Hell notes, paper houses, cars, etc., are burnt to be used in the after life.

The coffin lies buried for up to ten years. Then the bones are dug up, cleaned and put into an earthenware pot. The bones now need a good and lucky burial place. A geomancer – a special person who knows about the power of the earth and waters – is called in to choose a site. It must have good views of water and have good winds blowing over it. This is called feng shui – wind/

water. Once the site has been found, an elaborate curved tomb is built and at last the bones are laid to rest. It is to the feng shui tomb that the family will come once a year at Ching Ming festival, to make offerings to the ancestors.

▲ *At a Chinese funeral, paper models of houses, cars, TVs, Bank of Hell money and so on are burnt to provide the dead person with these things in the after life.*

Christian

DEATH RITES

FOR CHRISTIANS, death is the end and yet not the end. They know that it is the end of the person's life on earth, but believe that the soul goes on to an after life. In this, they are following the teachings of Jesus, who not only rose from the dead, but returned to show his friends that God gives life after death.

It is difficult to say what the after life is like. Jesus did not say much about it. Some Christians believe that, straight after death, the soul goes to be judged by God. If the person lived a good life and believed in God, then the soul goes to Heaven. If they were very bad they go to fiery Hell. For some, there is a half-way house called Purgatory. This is where people who have not been too bad go. They spend a long time here to make up for the bad things they did, then they go to Heaven.

Other Christians believe that the souls stay in the bodies and that they will come to life again on the Day of Judgement when God will end the world and judge everyone, dead or living. Yet others do not believe in a fiery Hell – or in any kind of place as punishment. They believe the good live with God and the bad simply cease to exist.

What happens . . .

Catholics, just before death, are given Extreme Unction – they are anointed with oil by a priest to bless them. The funeral usually takes place within four to five days. The body is washed and dressed in normal clothes. In some communities the body is laid out with candles at the head and feet and members of the family sit throughout the days and nights beside it.

When the coffin approaches the

Death

church, followed by mourners dressed in black, the priest meets the coffin and escorts it into the church with these words: 'I am the Resurrection and the Life says the Lord'. The priest will give a brief talk about the person and the prayers speak not only of sorrow but also of joy and hope because of life after death.

The body is then either buried, or burned at a crematorium with more prayers being said. If the body has been cremated, the ashes are either scattered over a garden of remembrance or are buried with, say, a rose bush planted above.

Flowers, many made into wreaths or Christian symbols, are carried on the coffin or beside it and placed on the grave.

▼ *Grave-diggers prepare for a Christian funeral. Many Christian families still prefer to bury their dead rather than have a cremation.*

Hindu

DEATH RITES

HINDUS BELIEVE that, unless you have lived an extremely good life – in which case you go to join the supreme God, Brahma – you will be reborn on earth in a new body. The soul, called atman, is given a new life and body as reward or punishment for the kind of life he or she led before. We go through many, many rebirths and should try to be better every time until eventually we do not have to come back.

To help this improvement, there are sixteen special ceremonies in life, called samskara. The final one is cremation. Because it is only the soul (the atman) which is important, the body is burned after death, because it is not needed anymore. It is also felt that death makes those near it unclean. So the mourners stay at home and do not go out to meet people until all the ceremonies have finished.

What happens . . .

The dead body is wrapped in a new cloth – the shroud, and a piece of gold or silver is placed in the mouth and sometimes on the eyes as well. The coffin is then taken, in procession, to the funeral pyre – a big bonfire of wood. In Britain the coffin will go to a crematorium. The body is burnt, using ghee (a kind of Indian butter) to help the flames. The eldest son stands by the pyre or near to the furnace of the crematorium. Prayers and readings from Hindu scriptures such as the Bhagavad Gita are recited while the body burns. They express the belief in reincarnation: 'For to one that is born, death is certain; and to one that dies, birth is certain. Therefore do not grieve over what is unavoidable.'

Three days later the ashes are collected and, if it is possible,

▲ *At a Hindu funeral in India the coffin is carried to the funeral pyre to be burned. Then the ashes will be scattered on the sacred river, Ganges.*

scattered onto the sacred river Ganges. In Britain it is common for the ashes to be sent to India to be scattered on the Ganges.

Finally, ten or twelve days after the cremation, comes the kriya ceremony. Offerings of riceballs – pindas – are made by the eldest son, followed by rice cooked in milk. These are offered not just to the relative who has just died, but to all deceased relatives and ancestors of the family.

After this final act of the sixteenth samskara, the family is no longer considered polluted and unclean by the death and normal life can start again. It is believed that the soul has now been reborn so the old person no longer exists in any form.

Death

Jewish

DEATH RITES

IT IS DIFFICULT to give a clear picture of what Jews believe happens to the soul after death. Jews believe that the soul lives on after the body has died, but what happens to it after death is often talked about and there is some disagreement.

Some Jews believe that the soul goes immediately to God and dwells there, watching what happens on earth. Others say that the souls remain with the dead bodies waiting for the Final Day. On that day, the Messiah, the special servant of God, will come to earth and the dead will rise, bodies and all, and come to the Messiah. This is known as the Resurrection. Yet others have taught that the soul comes back to earth at every death, but in a new body. This is called transmigration of souls.

Traditional Jews never burn (cremate) the bodies at death – in case the souls need the bodies for the Resurrection. More liberal or reform Jews do practise cremation as they believe more in an eternal life for the soul.

What happens . . .
If possible, the dying person will die with the words of the great prayer, Shema Yisrael, on his or her lips: 'Hear O Israel the Lord our God is One God'.

Once the person is declared dead, the body is washed, anointed with spices and wrapped in a white linen sheet – the shroud. Burial must take place as soon as possible.

To show their sadness, the main mourners make a cut in their coat – this is to recall former days when the mourners ripped their garments.

The coffin is taken from the synagogue to the Jewish cemetery. No flowers are allowed. After a short service, and a talk about the dead person by the Rabbi, the coffin is taken to the grave. Friends and family shovel earth onto it while the son or closest male relative reads the kaddish – a prayer of glory to God.

For the next seven days the family is in full mourning – shiva. Friends will look after them and kaddish is said every day. After shiva, mourners try to return to normal life – but they have a period of thirty days when they must not go to any entertainment. Finally for eleven months the kaddish must be said daily.

On the anniversary of the death, a 24-hour candle is lit, often in the synagogue, in memory of the dead person and the grave is visited, usually around Jewish New Year.

Muslim

DEATH RITES

MUSLIMS BELIEVE in life after death: the angel of death comes and carries the soul to a special 'place', which is not like being on earth. This is where the souls will wait for the Day of Judgement. This 'waiting state' is called Barzakh. Here, a thousand years seems less than a day.

The day of Judgement will be the end of the earth. On that day the earth will be destroyed and Allah will come to judge everyone, dead or living. Those who have lived good lives will go to Paradise, where they will live in a beautiful garden and enjoy all that is good. Hell awaits those who lived mean or bad lives. Here they will live in fire and suffer forever. Because the Holy Book, the Qur'an, teaches that the dead will have their bodies restored on the Day of Judgement, cremation is forbidden.

What happens . . .
When people are dying, they should be surrounded by their family and friends who will read from the Qur'an (Holy Book), particularly from Surah (chapter) 97, which answers basic questions about life after death and the Day of Judgement. If the dying person is able, he or she should say the Creed of Islam, the Ash-shahada: 'There is no God but Allah and Muhammad is the Prophet of Allah.'

Once the person has died, the body must be buried as soon as possible. It is washed three times using soap, washing first the ears, nose, mouth, head, feet, hands and forearms. (These are the parts which Muslims wash before prayer.) The body is then anointed with perfume and wrapped in three pieces of white cotton as a shroud, called a kafan.

At the mosque, the coffin lies in front of the Imam who faces Mecca. Together the Imam and congregation say the funeral prayer – the Salat ul-Janazah. Unlike normal prayer times, the congregation remains standing throughout. The Salat ul-Janazah has within it prayers asking for Allah's mercy and forgiveness for the dead person.

The burial must take place in a Muslim cemetery or Muslim part of a normal cemetery. It is usual for the grave to be covered with a raised mound of earth, but large gravestones or monuments are discouraged. Families mourn for periods up to three days. It is common to read through the Qu'ran as a source of comfort.

When people hear of a death, there is a common saying which expresses some of the fundamental ideas of Islam. They say: 'To God we belong and to him we return'.

Sikh

DEATH RITES

SIKHS BELIEVE that when the soul leaves the body it has to go through many rebirths and new bodies until, at long last, it is able to stop having to be reborn and returns to God. To have been born a human shows that the soul is on the way to returning to God. It is possible therefore that, when a Sikh dies, the soul will go to God and not be reborn, if the life has been good and God gives his grace. For those souls judged not good enough yet, rebirth takes place, sometimes after a time of rest or of testing.

Because of these beliefs, Sikhs are not too sad when someone dies, especially after a long life. Mourning is not encouraged because it seems to go against the hopes and beliefs which Sikhism teaches.

What happens . . .
As a Sikh lies dying, the family and friends will read the Hymn of Peace – the Sukhmani written by Guru Arjan, which teaches that all blessings come to us from God's grace. If the dying people can, they will try to say 'Waheguru' – 'Wonderful God' – just before they die.

The body is washed and dressed again with the five symbols – the five Ks of Sikhism (bracelet; long hair; comb; kirpan-sword and shorts) on the body. The body is taken first to the temple – gurdwara – but is not taken inside. It is then taken to be burned – usually in the West in a crematorium. The men of the family watch over the cremation. Following a prayer for the peace of the soul, the evening or bedtime prayer (the Sohila) is said. The family and friends return to the gurdwara where a speech about the dead person is given, followed by hymns and prayers. The service ends with the sharing of the karah parshad – the special food. It is also common for there to be a feast in the langar (free kitchen) and for gifts to be given to the poor or the gurdwara.

The ashes are collected the next day and scattered, with flowers, on to a running stream or river.

For ten days after the funeral, the Guru Granth Sahib (Holy Book) is read right through, in the home. On the last day, the passage describing Guru Amar Das' death is read. Friends will call during this time to help the family settle back into normal life.

▲ *The Sikhs cremate their dead. The body is dressed, in death as in life, with the five Ks and the men of the family watch over the cremation. The ashes are collected and scattered, with flowers, on to running water.*

Buddhist Rites

Buddhist

RITES OF PASSAGE

IT IS VERY DIFFICULT to talk of rites of passage within Buddhism. Buddhism is based on the life style of the monks and nuns who live in the religious communities – the Sangha. They do not marry – indeed the Buddha himself left his wife and child to seek Enlightenment.

Buddhism also teaches (particularly in its Theravada form) that there is no soul. So Buddhists do not feel, religiously, that there is much to make a fuss about either at birth or death.

However, this does not apply to ordinary people. For them, Buddhism is a tremendous ideal which they can share in, but not really be part of. So, in many cultures, the older pre-Buddhist rites of passage, gods and beliefs have survived and it is these which people use to celebrate birth, marriage and death. It is customary to invite Buddhist monks to come and share in the food and perhaps to preach a sermon or recite one of the Buddhist scriptures (sutras). But the actual ceremonies are pre-Buddhist. Buddhist lay–people can gain merit by giving food to the Sangha and by listening to the sermons or sutras, and this is certainly of considerable importance. But what goes on during the main rites is not really connected with the Buddha's teaching.

For instance, in Thai Buddhism, the ceremonies for birth owe more to Hinduism than to Buddhism. When the baby is born, the umbilical cord is kept, salted and placed in an earthenware pot which is then buried under a tree. The baby is put into a special cradle; if it is a boy, the cradle will have books, tools, etc, in it. If it is a girl, the cradle has needles, threads, etc.

After a month comes the main ceremony. The baby's hair is cut

off because it is seen as unclean. Around the baby's wrists are tied sacred threads. Thais believe that everyone has a guardian spirit, called a 'Khwan', and that the sacred thread helps the Khwan to settle down and feel at home.

Sometimes for good luck, monks will be asked to name the child and food is always given to the monks.

The only ceremony which Buddhists do have is ordination. In Thailand and Burma for instance, it is common for all boys aged between ten and twenty (or sometimes younger) to go and spend some time in a Buddhist monastery. In Burma, the boys re-enact the story of how the wealthy luxury-living Prince Siddhatha became the Buddha. It is a very special Buddhist event, this initiation or ordination into the Sangha, and constitutes the only major Buddhist rite of passage.

When it comes to marriages, monks and nuns will be invited but they do not marry the couples, but simply attend and maybe

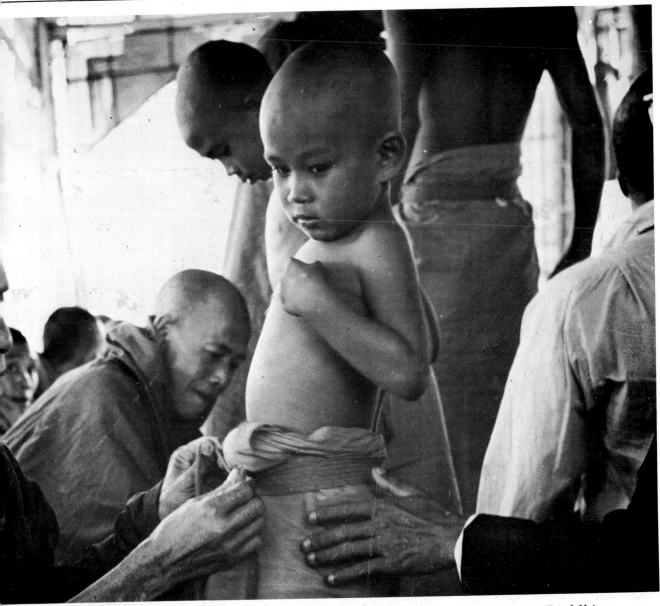

preach as well. The ceremony is usually very simple. In Sri Lanka and Thailand it does not take place in a religious building. The vows in Sri Lanka are of a simple descriptive nature, for example: 'Towards my wife I undertake to love and respect her, be kind and considerate, be faithful, delegate domestic management, provide gifts to please her'. In Burma the couple will, however, repeat the creed of Buddhism: 'I take refuge in the Buddha, the Dhamma (his teachings) and the Sangha'.

Funerals are also similar to the Hindu kind. The body is burned and the ashes either scattered or buried. Monks will usually preach about what Buddha taught regarding existence after death, but there is little of the ceremony which really reflects this teaching.

Buddhism is a complex and challenging belief. It is able to live alongside very different beliefs and to absorb them into its teaching. The loyalty of lay Buddhists to Buddhism is very

▲ *In certain Buddhist countries (such as Burma and Thailand) young boys spend a short while living in a monastery as novice monks. Here a young boy is dressed in the distinctive robes of a Buddhist monk.*

great. But when it comes to the rites of passage, they supplement the stern truths of Buddhism with the vibrance and symbolism of earlier beliefs.

In the Classroom

THE GROWTH of a multi-faith and multi-cultural society has been a source of enormous stimulation to many teachers. In both primary and secondary schools it has helped free religious ideas and stories from the traditional narrow bonds of 'Scripture' and 'RK' and has meant that myths, language, symbols, art, music, festivals, passions, costumes, customs and concepts from a great diversity of cultures and faiths are now to be encountered in the classroom. It is obviously impossible and unnecessary to give examples of classroom work on every festival and rite. I have simply taken one festival and one rite for primary and the same for secondary as examples of the tremendous range of possibilities for classroom work and discussion which arise from a multi-faith society such as ours.

But first a few basic hints. Just because children come from a particular faith background, don't assume that they are instant experts in all the theological/mythological dimensions of that faith! It is far better to ask them to help you make contact with their parents and/or with their religious leaders so that, between you, you can find out about what is going on, what it really means to that family, community and, ultimately, child. If possible, get the children to bring materials into the classroom or, even better, arrange a visit to the temple, synagogue, etc, with the children acting as guides. But it is important that, if you are going to visit a place of worship, you should check with your local RE Centre, Adviser and/or Community Relations office to see if this particular place is the best one to visit. A bad visit is a disaster.

Moreover there are some very real problems in just visiting places of worship, especially when they are not in use (which is the usual situation in the middle of the day during the week). They can often come over as dead, unused museums rather than living centres of faith. It is this lack of a sense of the place of worship being at the centre of ordinary life which makes me hesitant about the value of one-off visits. One way of overcoming this problem is by the construction or use of religious urban trails. For some time, schools have used the countryside as their classroom with nature trails. More recently, the growth of town trails or urban trails has made use of the urban environment. In the last few years, the religious urban trail has been pioneered in Manchester.

Primary school

Festival. *Eid ul-Fitr.* How is Eid ul-Fitr's date chosen? What sort of a calendar is used? Here is a fascinating starting point for a class project on Eid and Ramadan. Once the calendar has been explored, this leads to the Hajj – the pilgrimage, and to questions about Mecca. Where is Mecca? Which wall of the classroom would be the Qibla wall (the wall facing Mecca)? From such geographical, historical and chronological work, the class could look at the two religious activities which are integral to the festival and which are the basic aspect of so many festivals – fasting and celebrating. Why do people fast? What are they celebrating? The vast array of Eid cards which are on sale provide plenty of resources for children to create their own Eid cards – always remembering the prohibition on images of Allah and Muhammad.

There is also the theme of charity – zakat. Why is it given? Do other faiths have gift ceremonies? How do they differ? Finally a child or

◄ *A group of children enact the Passover meal in school. Using the special service book, the Haggadah, they can go through all the stories, questions and special foods which make up the Passover meal. Through this event, even non-Jewish children can enter into the spirit and story of Passover.*

opens the door to sympathetic exploration of the faith itself, its holy books, worship and beliefs. If you are doing world studies, for instance, compare what happens in your local Muslim community with what occurs in Pakistan or Bangladesh. If you are in a church school it might be important to explore the somewhat stormy history of Muslim/Christian relationship such as the Crusades, to see how things have changed or ought to change.

Rites. *Chinese birth rites.* Many teachers do projects on Babies, Birthdays or Myself. By using the beliefs which lie behind the various celebrations associated with birth, a variety of themes can be drawn out. For instance, using the Chinese ceremonies and concepts you can start by looking at ideas of time. A Chinese baby, born the day before Chinese New Year, is two Chinese years old by the time he or she is a day old! The Chinese don't celebrate individual birthdays – what does that bring out about the children's own understanding of birthdays? The fear of evil spirits stealing the baby – was this caused by the large number of babies which died (and which in poorer areas still do die) while they were very young? The giving of different names at different times – what does this draw out from the children about the power of names? Why are boys often seen as being more important than girls? Here's

adult describing what Ramadan or Eid ul-Fitr is like would give other children a powerful insight into the festival. Perhaps the

class could prepare an assembly on the festival introducing the various strands mentioned above.

Needless to say, any festival

▲ *Before going out on a religious trail, a class of children study the trail guide.*

a big and lively topic! All this besides the normal material on families preparing for the baby; the excitement; sibling rivalry; the creation of new life and so on. And there is always food! Try making the 'red' eggs – perhaps the local Chinese take-away will help here.

Many families have their own traditions and rituals as well. Perhaps, when using this book, you can talk about their family customs to build a more diverse picture of how rites of passage are celebrated.

Secondary school

Festival. *Janmashtami.* As so much depends upon the sort of overall syllabus which the teacher has developed in RE, Humanities or General Studies, I will simply try to illustrate the diversity of issues which a study

of Janmashtami might open up for a class.

Firstly there is mythology. The stories of Krishna, with Janmashtami providing the birth, offer a splendid introduction to myth, saga and epic. How were stories told and developed? What is the power of the stories? What are the meanings of the symbols and characters? For older groups, what does Jung have to say about such stories? Secondly, the theology of Krishna. Krishna is an avatar of Vishnu. Here lies a whole exploration of godhead, deity, Hindu beliefs, incarnation and so on. A fascinating area lies in the comparison of birth stories between, for instance, Krishna, Buddha, Jesus and Muhammad. Such a study does a great deal to clarify the respective understandings of God and Humanity which underpin these faiths. Thirdly the eternal theme of good versus evil. Why is there evil? How can it be handled? Why is there suffering? Fourthly there is the issue of

religious experience. To be guests at Janmashtami celebrations at the local Hindu temple is to come a little closer to understanding the power of religion. To listen to the chanting, singing, and clapping; to share in the arti ceremony; to receive gifts of fruit is to begin to appreciate how religion moves the ordinary Hindu.

Finally there is the spin-off issue of the Hare Krishna movement and its appeal, predominantly to young people from non-Hindu backgrounds. Often cast as a 'sect' – subject of the occasional sensational news item – what do ordinary Hindus make of it? Why do young people join? What is the basis for the media attacks? What is the movement's significance within the sociology of religion?

Rites. *Jewish death rites.* Again, I am making the assumptions outlined at the start of the festival section above. The following issues could be raised when studying Jewish death rites. Firstly, the variety of understandings of the after-life. It is not a simple cut-and-dried set of ideas. This raises important questions about the nature of religious language and the development of beliefs. It also introduces the whole area of the variety of beliefs that people can hold, even when they seem to contradict each other – and here a cross reference to Chinese death rites would be instructive. Secondly, the concept of an end of time, a judgement day, is very important. What is the purpose of Divine Creation? How and why will it end? Is the nuclear threat a form of Last Day? What ethical and moral implications are there in these ideas? Thirdly, the question of death. What is death – is it the end? What of euthanasia? What about ghosts – dybbuks in certain Jewish traditions? Fourthly, what has death to say about life? Fifthly, why mourn? Is it helpful to have public mourning and ascribed times of mourning? What is the social rôle of mourning?

I hope this brief outline indicates some of the vast arenas of thought, experience and questions which festivals and rites of passage throw up. We live in exciting times as our society becomes more and more cosmopolitan. Through the high days and holy days we can enter in, albeit briefly, to another world, another way of living, another way of thinking.

A religious trail takes children and teachers out into a part of their city which is predominantly Jewish, Chinese, Muslim, etc. Through careful and co-ordinated work with members of those communities, the children are offered the opportunity to be the guests of a particular faith or ethnic community for a day.

They are able to visit community centres and shops selling foods or other articles associated with that group. They may have the opportunity to learn how to read a few words in Hebrew or Chinese or Punjabi. They will be strangers in their own city, meeting and learning from a group who have made their home in that area. Then, to visit a place of worship (perhaps in the company of a group or family from that community) makes sense. The children can see it as the worshipping centre of a wide community which eats, talks, laughs, trades and cares – and, in that setting, the place of worship becomes a significant element of the overall picture.

Few Centres offer ready-made religious urban trails, but they are not difficult to construct. For urban primary schools, a class project on their own area would probably throw up a wide range of religious centres and activities. The children's parents could help to make these accessible to the class. A term's class project of this kind can provide a stimulating range of insights and experiences.

In the secondary school, children working on a CSE project or General Studies group could perhaps undertake to construct a trail around one community. It is essential that the work is done with the community's full agreement and that you do not start to treat the community as a zoo. But, with sensitivity and care, doors can be opened into the lifestyle of a religious group (and that group could well be Christians). In this way a breadth of insight and sharing can be achieved which is unlikely to be matched in a straightforward visit to a 'place of worship'.

In the preceding notes I have not made any special mention of assemblies but, obviously, those schools who see assembly as an occasion to share and celebrate the diversity of our society can make good use of the material in this book. Likewise, I have said little about art or music because the ideas themselves nearly all have possibilities in these areas and there are numerous resources for that.

▼ *A religious urban trail is not difficult to construct. This is part of a trail guide produced for Manchester children.*

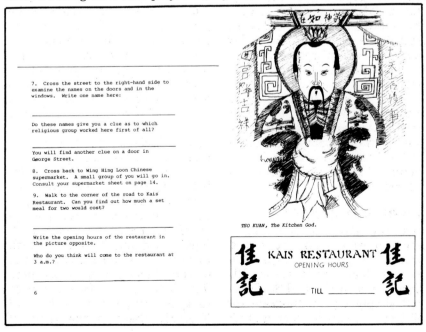

TSO KUAN, The Kitchen God.

Source List

Where relevant, the addresses of organisations are given when they are first mentioned. (Prices are not given as they go out of date so rapidly.)

General books

Charing D. et al, *Comparative Religions*, Blandford (1982).
Cole O. *Five Religions in the Twentieth Century*, Hulton (1982).
Cole O. *World Religions – a Teacher's Handbook*, Commission for Racial Equality.
Ferguson J. *Religions of the World*, Lutterworth (1978).
Foy W. *Man's Religious Quest*, Croom Helm (1978).
Larousse World Mythology, Hamlyn (1973).
Ling T. *A History of Religion, East and West*, Macmillan (1968).
Smart N. *Background to the Long Search*, BBC (1976).

Series of books and audio-visual aids

Please note, in most cases the series vary considerably in quality between one book in the series and another.
Peerless A. and B. *Slide Sets* on major religions, (22 King's Avenue, Minnis Bay, Birchington, Kent CT7 9QL).
Argus Major World Religions, Argus Communications. Large audio-visual packs.
The Family in Britain series, REP.
Library of the World's Myths and Legends, Newnes (2nd edition, 1982).
Living Religions series, Ward Lock Educational.

SHAP mailing. Irregular but excellent mailing on world religions. Shap Working Party (7 Alderbrook Road, Solihull, West Midlands B91 1NH).
Strands series, A&C Black.
The Way of . . . series, Hulton.
Understanding your Neighbour series, Lutterworth.

Particular religions

Buddhism

Ling T. *The Buddha*, Penguin (1981).
Naylor D. *Thinking about Buddhism*, Lutterworth;
Topic Folder 5, Buddhism, CEM (1979). (Christian Education Movement; Chester House, Pages Lane, London N10 1PR.)
Wichagonrakul P. *The Life of the Buddha*, Sacred Trinity Centre, (1983). (Chapel Street, Salford M3 7AJ.)

Chinese

Baker H. *Ancestral images; Ancestral images Again; More Ancestral Images*. SOAS (School of Oriental and African Studies, University of London, Malet Street, London WC1) (1979-82).
Needham J. *Science and Civilization in China*, abridged version. Vol. 1. Cambridge (1956).
Palmer M. et al. *The Chinese Community in Manchester*, teacher's notes, Sacred Trinity Centre (1982).

Christianity

The CEM have a wide range of booklets in their current catalogue. Likewise, Lion publications have a good selection. The Mary Glasgow Publications' *Christianity* audio-visual pack provides a vast amount of information (1983).

Hinduism

O'Flaherty W. *Hindu Myths*, Penguin.
Sen K. *Hinduism*, Penguin (1971).
Zaehner R. *Hinduism*, OUP.
Bahree P. *The Hindu World*, Macdonald Educational (1982).

Islam

Tames R. *Approaches to Islam*, John Murray.
The Islamic Foundations (3-7 Keythorpe Street, Leicester) has a good list of books and materials, as have Invicta Books, (162 Coppice Street, Oldham).
The Muslim Information Service at 233 Seven Sisters Road, London, is another useful source.

Judaism

The Jewish Education Bureau (Sacred Trinity Centre, Chapel Street, Salford M3 7AJ) has a vast array of books, audio-visual aids and artefacts for sale in their current catalogue. Highly recommended.
Charing D. *The Jewish World*, Macdonald Educational (1983).
Epstein I. *Judaism*, Penguin (1959).
Unterman A. *Jews*, RKP (1981).

Sikhism

Cole O. and Sambhi P. *The Sikhs*, RKP (1978).
McLeod W. *The Way of the Sikh*, Hulton.
Winstanley C. and Singh D. *Sikhism – Living a Faith*, audio-visual pack, Sacred Trinity Centre (1982).

Festivals

Books

Dargue W. *Assembly Stories from Around the World*, Oxford (1983).
SHAP calendar of religious festivals (issued annually). Shap mailings.
Thomas P. *Festivals and Holidays of India*, (Books from India, Museum Street, London WC1).

Series

Annual Festivals, sets of wall charts, Pictorial Charts, (27 Kirchen Road, West Ealing, London W13 0UD).
Festivals, audio-visual pack, Mary Glasgow Publications (1982).
Festivals, series of separate booklets on major festivals, RMEP (1982).

Rites of Passage

Books

Is Death the End? CEM (1979).
Prickett J. *Initiation Rites*, Lutterworth.
Prickett J. *Death*, Lutterworth.

Series

Rites of Passage, audio-visual pack, Mary Glasgow Publications (1979).
Rites of Passage, sets of wall charts, Pictorial Charts (1983).

▲ *Some of the titles in the comprehensive* Living Religions *series from Ward Lock Educational.*

Index

Picture Credits

Picture research by Jan Croot

We are grateful to the following people for supplying the photographs on the pages listed.

Front Cover: Dragon Boat, Hong Kong Tourist Association
Back Cover: Hindu wedding, Ann and Bury Peerless

Hugh Baker: 74
Barnaby's Picture Library: 24, 62, 63, 66, 76
Cameo: 71
Camera Press: 6 (left), 15, 20, 57, 80
Catholic Pictorial: 61
Courtauld Institute: 10
Michael Lindsay Edwards: 7, 8, 33, 51, 55, 56, 57, 64, 70, 79, 84
Egg Marketing Board: 21
Werner Forman Archive: 46
Stanley Gibbons: 2
Government of India Tourist Office: 13, 37, 50
Richard and Sally Greenhill: 4, 11, 54, 67, 68
Hong Kong Government Office: 41, 55
Hong Kong Tourist Association: 5, 16, 17, 38, 40
Israel Government Tourist Office: 48
Jewish Chronicle: 28, 43
Jewish Museum/Warburg Institute: 44
Manchester Evening News: 53
Mansell Collection: 29, 52
Middle East Photographic Archive: 23
Ann and Bury Peerless: 32, 47, 69, 77
Popperfoto: 72
David Richardson: 7 (left), 27, 35, 59, 60, 73
Harry Small: 83
Juliette Soester: 6 (right), 42, 45, 49, 58
Topham Picture Library: 19, 34, 39
Victoria and Albert Museum: 9, 14, 17, 18, 26, 30, 31, 36